Praise for *The Dad Difference*

"*The Dad Difference* is the right book at the right time! It comes when men's roles are being rethought and students' mental health is in crisis. The authors are both seasoned educators and bring their personal and professional experiences to bear in practical ways. They cite pertinent research and provide valuable tools to enable educators to actively invite dads and father figures into their students' in-school lives for the good of students, educators, dads, and the entire family."

—**Allan Shedlin,** founder & president, DADvocacy Consulting Group

"*The Dad Difference* is a timely book that reminds us that a father's presence is necessary and can be transformational. This book offers research and real-life examples of the positive effects that engaged fathers have not only on their own children but also on the greater community."

—**Elfreda Massie, PhD,** former superintendent of schools and author

"*The Dad Difference* urges schools to evaluate how their systems influence father engagement, either restricting or enabling its full potential. Dr. Deborah Higdon and Dr. Chacko Abraham advance beyond symbolic involvement by offering research-based, practical strategies that immediately strengthen partnerships. This book provides leaders, educators, and families with tools to foster more accountable and inclusive school cultures, thereby enhancing student outcomes and addressing intergenerational patterns in the present."

—**James C. Rodríguez, MSW,** president & CEO, Fathers & Families Coalition of America

“Fatherhood is a calling that extends beyond the home into schools, where children spend much of their formative time. This book highlights the vital role fathers play while calling schools to be proactive partners, fostering stronger families and more connected communities. It offers practical guidance for building meaningful collaboration that helps children thrive.”

—**Bishop Henry Hearns,** mayor emeritus,
City of Lancaster, California

“As a law enforcement officer for almost three decades, I have seen the often disastrous results when fathers are not present in the lives of their children. This book should be required reading for all primary school educators and anyone, including law enforcement, who work with children in both recreational and educational arenas. I hope this work inspires men to stand in the gap as mentors where fathers are absent.”

—**Shibu Philipose,** deputy chief of police,
City of Takoma Park, Maryland

“*The Dad Difference* offers inspiration and practical encouragement for educators and holds great promise for both fathers and the children whose futures are strengthened when fathers fully engage.”

—**Mark A. Martin, PhD,** principal,
Martin & Associates Strategic Management Consulting

THE DAD DIFFERENCE

CHACKO ABRAHAM
DEBORAH R. HIGDON

THE DAD DIFFERENCE

HOW AND WHY TO INVITE FATHERS INTO YOUR SCHOOL

Arlington, Virginia USA

iste+ascd™

2111 Wilson Boulevard, Suite 300 • Arlington, VA 22201 USA
Phone: 800-933-2723 or 703-578-9600
Website: www.ascd.org • Email: member@ascd.org
Author guidelines: www.ascd.org/write

Richard Culatta, *Chief Executive Officer;* Genny Ostertag, *Managing Director, Book Acquisitions & Editing;* Stephanie Bize, *Acquisitions Editor;* Mary Beth Nielsen, *Director, Book Editing & Design;* Katie Martin, *Senior Editor;* Georgia Park, *Graphic Designer;* Emily Reed, *Senior Director, Publishing Operations;* Circle Graphics, *Typesetter;* Christopher Logan, *Senior Production Specialist;* Shajuan Martin, *E-Publishing Specialist*

All links in this book are correct as of the publication date below but may have become inactive or otherwise modified since that time. If you notice a broken link, email books@ascd.org; include "Link Update" in the subject line; and in the message, specify the link, the book title, and the page number on which the link appears.

PAPERBACK ISBN: 978-1-4166-3433-1 Product #125005 n5/26
PDF EBOOK ISBN: 978-1-4166-3434-8; see Books in Print for other formats.
Quantity discounts are available: email programteam@ascd.org or call 800-933-2723, ext. 5773, or 703-575-5773. For desk copies, go to www.ascd.org/deskcopy.

Library of Congress Cataloging-in-Publication Data

Names: Abraham, Chacko author | Higdon, Deborah R. author
Title: The dad difference : how and why to invite fathers into your school / Chacko Abraham, Deborah R. Higdon.
Description: Arlington, Virginia : ISTE+ASCD, [2026] | Includes bibliographical references and index.
Identifiers: LCCN 2026000652 (print) | LCCN 2026000653 (ebook) | ISBN 9781416634331 paperback | ISBN 9781416634348 pdf
Subjects: LCSH: Education--Parent participation | Father and child
Classification: LCC LB1048.5 .A27 2026 (print) | LCC LB1048.5 (ebook)
LC record available at https://lccn.loc.gov/2026000652
LC ebook record available at https://lccn.loc.gov/2026000653

35 34 33 32 31 30 29 28 27 26 1 2 3 4 5 6 7 8 9 10 11 12

THE DAD DIFFERENCE

Preface

It's a surprise to both of us—Chacko and Deborah—that we teamed up to write a book about dads and education. Here's how it began.

The year was 2020, and COVID-19 was in full swing. We had both registered for the first-ever BOND Academy conference—Chacko as a presenter and Deborah as an attendee. The pandemic had changed the conference to a 100-percent virtual event, and as sometimes happens in virtual conferences, technology threw a curveball. During Chacko's session, "Engaging Fathers in Education," his internet connection went down, leaving the attendees without a facilitator. Audience member Deborah, who had run a successful father engagement program at her school in Maryland, stepped up to fill the silence and answer some of her fellow attendees' questions. It took Chacko several minutes to reconnect. When he was back online, he was surprised to find not only that everyone was still there but that there was a woman leading the discussion and sharing practical tips on father engagement.

Our partnership grew from there, fueled by a shared belief that fathers are a valuable, underused resource in schools. From our different corners of the world, we both had noticed that dads were too often absent when it came to their children's learning and growth. We both had stories about school meetings where only mothers showed up, stories about fathers who wanted to be more present in their children's school but didn't know how to begin, and stories about educators who were not sure how to go about the work of father engagement.

That's how this book began—with a shared concern and a deep conviction that dads have a vital role to fulfill in their children's education. And by "dads" and "fathers," we mean any adult male role model in students' lives, not necessarily biological fathers.

In our roles as school administrators, we have seen the influence that father engagement, and the lack of father engagement, can have on students and the school environment. We have watched the shifts in key cultural beliefs on the topics of paternity leave, child custody, and men's role in child rearing. Today's fathers are taking on more nontraditional roles, with many stating that they are happy to be in these roles, happy to have time to be with their children, and most of all, happy for their children to have time with them. We believe conditions and trends are ripe for schools to team up with motivated fathers. Having seen how fathers in schools can serve as role models, leaders, and guardians of their children's development, we believe that a pivotal solution to several school challenges lies in father engagement.

In the pages that follow, we share stories, insights, and practical ideas that we hope will encourage educators to leverage the talents and support that students' fathers offer as present, committed, and engaged partners in their children's education. This isn't a lecture—it's an opportunity for you to extend invitations to them. Our hope is that every educator who reads these words will feel inspired and reminded that every father's presence holds a depth of meaning greater than anyone can truly comprehend.

We'd like to begin with a little bit about who we are and why we were called to this work.

Chacko's Story

My enlightenment about fatherhood began long before I understood the full breadth of the role fathers play in our lives. After my brother and I were born, my parents moved to the United States so that my mother could pursue a nursing career. This was an opportunity to succeed, a way for them to help their children's dreams come true. Unfortunately, my father was unable to reciprocate his professional license in the United States, so he took on a manual labor job to support us. Back in India, he had been a civil engineer; moving to America really meant starting over again. Looking back, I can see the profound sacrifice he made, which has helped to shape my understanding of fatherhood and education.

Several years into this job, my father was injured and forced to take disability leave, which he spent taking care of us at home. My sister was born around this time, so my father had three children to watch over while my mom was at work. Though a stay-at-home father was far from the cultural norm at the time, he contributed so much to our upbringing just by being there with us.

Both my parents thought it was important for us to have a strong religious base, so we regularly attended church, which gave me the opportunity to work with and connect with children. I began as an assistant Sunday school teacher and eventually was put in charge of the entire Sunday school program, overseeing the children as well as the teachers, when I was still a teenager. I also assisted with church youth programs, interacting with kids both in group settings and one-on-one. These interactions helped me understand the importance of teaching, guiding, and listening to children. It also sparked a passion for education.

I started my professional education career as a kindergarten teacher in a classroom of 12 students whose mothers were considerably more involved in their education than their fathers. It was the mothers, not the fathers, who usually attended parent–teacher conferences. I quickly realized that I was the only male role model many of my students spent time with on a daily basis. I often asked myself, "Where are the dads?" The absence of fathers from my students' academic lives stayed with me, igniting a deep sense of urgency and purpose. I was determined to understand why so many fathers were missing in action from their children's education. I felt driven to engage with them and bring them on board. The importance of the male role model has been reinforced consistently through the years when former students of mine have sought me out to spend time with me.

My own journey into fatherhood began as I was embarking on my first year as a school administrator. The role of assistant principal, like those of being a father and a supportive husband, brought with it expectations and challenges that required my full attention. My willingness to excel as an administrator meant leaving home very early in the morning and coming back late at night at the expense of time spent bonding with my son. Two years later, when my daughter was born, I began to realize that providing for my children financially was not sufficient. What they really needed from me was my presence in their lives. I believe this is true for all children.

Deborah's Story

I grew up in Western Pennsylvania with my parents, older brother, and two older sisters. I always thought that one day I would get married and have a family and live out the "normal" life I had planned. But it did not happen that way. I got married when I was 24. I had my son when I was 31. Unfortunately, my marriage did not last. When my son was

10 months old, I separated from his father and moved out of the state. I got divorced. I raised my son on my own.

As a single parent, I did everything in my power to provide for my son. I gave him a loving home, and I saved money and bought us a house in a good neighborhood with excellent schools. I was active in his life and in his school. I took us on trips out of the country and exposed him to cultural experiences. Everything I did was out of love for my son, but none of it could fill the gap he was feeling. In fact, it wasn't until I started writing this book and talked to him about it that I learned about the emotional weight he felt growing up without his father in the house. I knew my divorce had hurt him, but I had no idea how much. For many years, he had been hurting in silence.

When I first separated from my son's father, my parents told me to make sure I let his father and his side of the family have a relationship with my son. I didn't want to do it; I was angry and really wanted my son's father to feel some of the hurt that I was feeling due to the breakup of our marriage. I don't know why—probably out of the great respect I had for my parents—I listened to them and never kept my son away. However, his father chose not to be active in his life. He made a conscious choice not to engage as a parent, which hurt my son deeply. I was aware of this hurt but had no idea how deep it was. I did not realize that my smiling, joyful son was drowning in sorrow while trying to hide it all from me so I wouldn't hurt along with him. Had I known, I would have intervened and made sure there was a connection between him and his father.

One time, during a blizzard, my son and I stayed at my sister and brother-in-law's house so we wouldn't be stranded home alone. While we were there, my son slept in longer than normal. When I asked him why, he shared that he slept well because my brother-in-law was around to protect him from any intruders. He told me that he always slept with an "ear open" at home in case someone broke in, because as the "man of the house" his job was to protect me. I was shocked. I hadn't realized that my preteen son felt the need to protect me. Later, I found out that many boys from fatherless homes feel that they must always be prepared to defend their home.

I remarried when my son was 13 years old. Although he and his stepdad had a good relationship with each other, it wasn't enough to fill the void left by his absent father. In fact, seeing me with a man who showed him attention made his longing for his biological father worse. Reflecting over the years on my son's hurt has deepened my resolve to encourage the presence of fathers in their children's education. You'll learn more about the extensive work I have done in this area, as you read on. For now, suffice to say that I have seen first-hand what the absence or presence of fathers at school can mean for students . . . and the profound difference dads can make. Today, I am more motivated than ever to help change the narrative that fathers are "extras" rather than essential when it comes to parent engagement.

Fathers' Voices

Before writing this book, we interviewed fathers and got their perspectives on parental engagement. You'll find their authentic words woven throughout the chapters and presented in full in the Appendix. Except for minor edits for clarity, we have presented their quotes verbatim; in our minds, it would be a disservice to these fathers to sanitize their perspectives for the sake of readers' comfort. Sometimes the truth hurts, but it can also bring healing.

At the time of the interviews, the fathers had children ranging in age from newborns to high school students. Several were young men—friends of Deborah's son whom she'd known since they were in high school. All these dads spoke about their relationships with their own fathers, what they hoped to pass on or do differently with their children, and what expectations they had for interacting with their children's schools. We are also including some quotes from fathers who participated in father engagement programs and extend our gratitude to all these men for their honesty and openness.

How to Use This Book

We intend this book to be a flexible resource. If you are considering creating a father engagement program, this book can provide a blueprint for starting and maintaining one. If you need encouragement, you can reread what we say about our own passion for engaging fathers in their children's education or review the dads' words to remind yourself of why engagement matters so much. And if you're simply looking for additional strategies to engage fathers, you'll find those, too.

When research identifies practical, low-cost ways to improve students' academic, social, and emotional outcomes, educators must take action. Father engagement doesn't require a lot of money, but it does require time and commitment to change. Some of the engagement strategies you'll find in this book will be familiar to you; all of them are tried and true. We have used them ourselves in our schools, or we have seen them used successfully and are comfortable vouching for them. They can be adapted to fit elementary, middle, and high schools of any size. They can be the foundation of a new father engagement program or a way to refresh one that's well-established. They're also perfect if you're looking to retool general "parent engagement strategies" to be more dad focused and dad friendly.

However you choose to proceed, we hope you take the opportunity to help your students succeed by further engaging their fathers in their education. The results will be invaluable–for your school, your students, and their dads, too.

CHAPTER

Understanding the Impact of Fathers

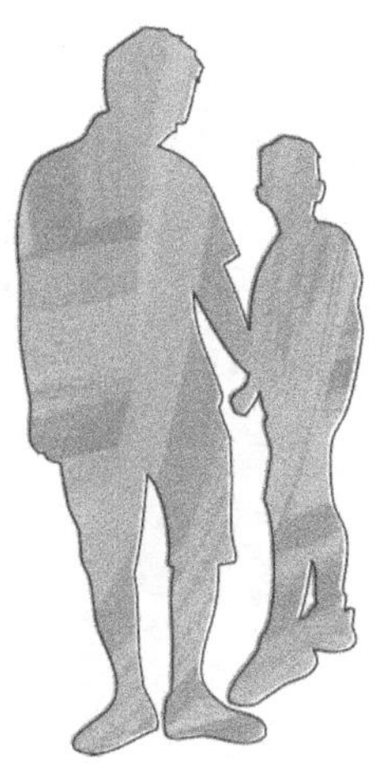

A meeting was scheduled at the middle school where I (Deborah) was an assistant principal. I was nervous and anxious because the meeting was only for fathers. The principal and I weren't even sure whether anyone would show up.

When the door opened, three men walked in. I could tell they were nervous, too. I thanked them as they entered and pointed to the area where we were going to sit. One of the men said, "These chairs are so small, I may not be able to fit in them." Everyone laughed. I asked, "When was the last time you were in a middle school?" To my surprise, he said, "About 15 years ago."

I asked the other fathers the same question. Their answers were similar: it had been at least 10 years since any of them had been in a middle school. One father said he had recently attended an event at his child's elementary school, where the seating was "even tighter." We all laughed, but behind my laugh I wondered: Why weren't these fathers in their children's schools more often? And as an administrator, why hadn't I reached out to them before? What could we, as a school community, do to keep fathers motivated and engaged with their children's learning? Could we collaborate with them to improve student outcomes, like behavior and achievement? To explore these questions, I dug into the evidence supporting family engagement and what decades of educational research have shown.

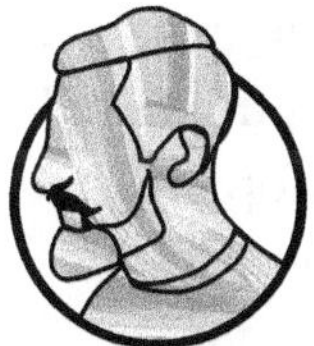

JOHN

"I want to be more visible with my children's teachers and more visible at their schools. I want the school to know that if I can be there, I will be there."

What the Research Shows

In 1966, the Johns Hopkins School of Education released the findings of one of the largest educational research studies ever conducted: *Equality of Educational Opportunity,* more commonly known as the Coleman Report in honor of its primary researcher, James S. Coleman. Coleman and his team of researchers collected data from 3,000 schools, 60,000 teachers, and nearly 600,000 students across the United States, with a focus on grades 1, 3, 6, 9, and 12. One major finding of the study was that students who have significant family support have better academic outcomes (Kiviat, 2000). Coleman and colleagues analyzed 737 pages of data and concluded, among other things, that family background trumped schooling as the primary determinant of educational success (Lowe, 2017).

Through the years, many researchers have replicated this study and have come to similar conclusions. Even though the Coleman Report was released in 1966, its analysis has held firm and been supported by educational research for nearly 60 years. In 1987, Anne T. Henderson determined that schools with strong parental involvement programs perform better than those that did not have such programs. In 1994, she collaborated with Nancy Berla to identify the following six family-related factors that influence student achievement:

1. The family makes critical contributions to student achievement from early childhood through high school.
2. When parents are involved at school, their children do better academically and are less likely to drop out.
3. When parents are involved in their children's education, they tend to send their kids to better schools.
4. Children do best when their parents are empowered to play four key roles in their learning: as teachers, supporters, advocates, and decision makers.

5. The more the relationship between family and school approaches a comprehensive, well-planned partnership, the higher student achievement becomes.
6. Families, schools, and community organizations all contribute to student achievement, and the best results emerge when all three work together. (Henderson & Berla, 1994)

In a 2018 interview, family engagement researcher Karen Mapp asserted that "family engagement—and I'm describing that as real, respectful partnerships between families and school staff—is as an absolutely essential ingredient—not only for student improvement but also for school improvement" (in Stringer, 2018, para. 8).

The benefits extend even further. For example:

- In a review of the literature on fatherhood, Astone and Peters (2014) found that engaged fathers were physically and emotionally healthier than other men and tended to live longer due to engaging in fewer risky behaviors. What's more, fathers' engagement in their sons' upbringing also is associated with reduced involvement in drugs, truancy, and criminal behavior for fathers *and* sons (Garbarino, 1999; Pollack, 2000). Note that these studies did not address the effects of father engagement on daughters.
- According to Green and colleagues (2014), sexually active adolescent teen girls who perceived their fathers to be distant or angry experienced more emotional and behavioral problems than those who had positive relationships with their fathers.
- Research by The Fatherhood Project (2023) found that children who have positive relationships with their fathers also have higher levels of sociability, confidence, and self-control, which in turn lead to better performance and fewer behavioral issues in school.

- Fathers who are routinely engaged in their children's schools tend to develop informal mentoring groups and build relationships with other students (Boberiene, 2013), helping to foster those students' social and emotional development. In schools dominated by female educators, these may be the only times some students see males as role models, leaders, and guides (Tsoi-A-Fatt, 2010).

Parental Engagement and the No Child Left Behind Act

The No Child Left Behind Act of 2001 emphasizes the role of parents in school partnerships. The act requires school administrators to ensure that school climates promote positive relationships that motivate parents, staff, and students. It also recommends that educators do the following:

- Clearly identify specific ways that parents can support their children's learning, such as by volunteering in the classroom, helping with homework, and taking part in decisions about their children's education.
- Help parents understand topics covered in their children's classes so they can assist with their children's education; and
- Educate faculty and staff on how to communicate, coordinate, and implement parental programs and build connections between home and school.

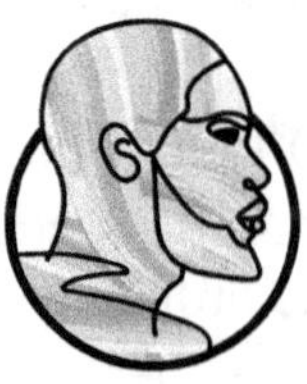

SAMUEL

"I didn't have a father—my own father—to check up on me with grades. I think that that played a role [in my life]. Granted, I had a tremendous mom who was amazing. She made sure I had my

grades right. She put the load on that! But there were many times when I wished I could have had a dad to check up on my grades and make sure. Like, "Hey! How are your grades doing?" and kind of put that hand down. But when I was a child, and even now as an adult, I did have great father figures [in] my uncles and some of my friends' dads. They really stepped up for me. Now that I am a father, I use the tools that I learned from my uncles and from some of my friends' dads to guide me."

Involvement Versus Engagement

Parental involvement and parental engagement may sound like the same thing, but it's more helpful to think of them as different sides of the same coin. You cannot have one without the other. They both describe participation but differ in role, motivation, and intensity.

Parental *involvement* refers to parents taking part in activities that are predetermined by the school. In terms of presence, they attend events, but do not plan them. Volunteering to help in the classroom or chaperone a field trip would be examples of involvement—taking part in a larger beneficial activity. Although these contributions are valuable and *can* lead to full parental engagement, they are not, in themselves, full engagement. Some parents may find them fulfilling, but other parents may hope for more or bristle at their limited impact.

Parental *engagement* takes the role parents play in school to a higher level and requires a deeper practical and emotional commitment. Where involvement may be driven by obligation or duty, engagement comes from connection and personal investment. When schools engage parents, they bring them in as part of the school's decision-making process to improve student outcomes. Engagement is more intentional than involvement, requiring openness from both the school and the parents. Examples of parental engagement include joining a school improvement team or serving on a district's curriculum review committee (Annie E. Casey Foundation, 2023).

Despite evidence that when *fathers* participate in their children's school activities, there's a positive effect on the children's academic achievement, many schools' parental involvement efforts generally target mothers. There is no malice behind this "mother bias," and schools often aren't even aware that their outreach is geared more toward moms than dads. Still, intentionally or not, the impression conveyed is that schools are only comfortable communicating and engaging with female caregivers. The role that mothers play in student learning is undoubtedly critical, and we do not want to minimize its importance. Many mothers who work full-time still find ways to engage in school events and activities, reflecting societal expectations about their role in children's lives (Brooks & Hodkinson, 2022). They are usually the ones who drop off students in the morning and pick them up in the afternoon. They are the primary presence at PTA meetings, at school bake sales, and on field trips. Traditionally, it's been mothers who volunteer in classrooms and attend more school events, whereas fathers were usually only seen at Back-to-School Night, sports events, and graduations (Schoppe-Sullivan, 2017).

However, studies show that frequent and positive involvement by fathers, specifically, can support their children's cognitive development and social and emotional development and improve academic outcomes (McBride et al., 2005; McWayne et al., 2013). It's critical that *both* parents play an active role in their children's education. When schools list the mother first on forms, send emails primarily to moms, or schedule events without considering fathers' work hours, they reflect an approach that puts fathers last.

Where Are the Dads?

Just as there are all kinds of sociological factors that influence fathers' physical and emotional presence in their children's lives, there are myriad reasons for fathers' comparative absence in schools.

Historically, schools were predominantly taught and attended by men. It was only in the 19th century, when more women began to enter the workforce in caregiving roles, that teaching came to be seen as "women's work." It is not uncommon today to see schools where women make up most of the teaching staff and the majority of school administrators. Considering the lower status and pay afforded "women's work," this gender imbalance is likely deterring men from joining the profession, compounding a situation in which students' fathers generally are not go-to considerations for parent engagement. Some schools never ask fathers to volunteer for school functions. It's possible that female educators are more comfortable contacting, communicating with, and interacting with mothers than they are with fathers. What we do know for sure is that, historically, schools do not take an active role in facilitating fathers participating in the education of their children (McBride et al., 2005).

It doesn't help that many men have had their own negative experiences in school that undermines their interest and willingness to engage. This is especially true for men who attended schools where their race was not the dominant one. Some schools have alienated fathers so much that when they do reach out to them, the father's first response is "What has happened that is so bad that you are calling me?" The underrepresentation of fathers at school events, other than sports, has been going on for so long that staff are often surprised to see fathers attending functions. They are even more surprised to see fathers participating or volunteering in what has been thought of as "mothers' activities."

The Evolution of Parental Roles in Education

While there may not be as many men in education as there used to be, it's also true that men are a lot more involved in parenting today than they've ever been. Over the past three decades, fathers have become increasingly engaged with their children's development (Hohman-Marriott, 2011; Kotila & Dush, 2013), with changes in economic conditions having a major impact on their roles (Cullen et al., 2013). Many families now need to have both parents working outside the home, which means they also need to split child-rearing duties (Pleck, 2010). As a result, fathers are now more willing to care for their children and assist with day-to-day activities (Cullen et al., 2013; DeGarmo, 2010; Shreffler et al., 2011).

It's a change. For most of U.S. history, fathers were seen as the center of the family, responsible for providing their wives and children with financial, emotional, and spiritual support. The division of labor was clear: Fathers made the rules, and mothers enforced them; fathers brought home the food, and mothers cooked it; fathers worked outside the home and kept up with the news, and mothers kept to the home and stayed up-to-date on their children's lives. (Note that some mothers, especially those who were not white, performed this role in other people's homes in addition to their own.) In most households, the father was the final authority. These roles were reflected in popular culture, too: From the dawn of television through the 1980s, TV shows nearly always portrayed fathers as the head of the household. But around the early 1990s, more shows began to present fathers as minor presences or even in demeaning ways. Some media critics suggest that these portrayals mirrored a societal discomfort with shifting gender roles and the growing expectation for fathers to step up at home (Scharrer, 2020).

More recent media portrayals of fathers reflect interesting societal shifts. In her 2023 article "The Modern Dad Syndrome," Rachel Choi observes,

> There seems to be a significant difference between the old and new era of fathers and father figures. The archetypal father has developed from an unfeeling disciplinarian to the empathetic caregiver. Consequently, the very framework of masculinity has changed as well; men are slowly but surely no longer expected to be threatening, stoic, and distant, but are encouraged to be intimate and emotional. (para. 7)

Choi points out that we see evidence of this younger generations of fathers "representing a gentler, warmer, more intimately connected figure that a child can lean on—a trait previously attributed solely to women."

In media depictions, the father's role has broadened and become more complex. Today, fathers are commonly portrayed as emotional and actively involved in childcare, reflecting increasing cultural acceptance of coparenting and changing ideologies of masculinity (Kaufman, 2021; Miller, 2019). While stereotypical dads can still be found in sitcoms and advertisements, we see more fathers displaying a much more caring attitude and a desire to balance work and family responsibilities.

More recently, many fathers were thrust into the role of teachers due to the COVID-19 pandemic. When schools closed and classes went virtual, dads who were also stuck at home got a glimpse of how challenging teaching is. Around the same time, schools realized that a once-a-year survey to parents or a winter concert was not enough of a connection to support effective partnership in students' education. Schools needed to do more to get parents engaged. COVID-19 also uncovered that there are many fathers who stay at home with the children while the mother works. The number of stay-at-home dads rose from 4 percent before the pandemic to 23 percent at its height in 2021 (Fry, 2023).

Now fathers are more willing to assist with the day-to-day activities in their children's lives (Cullen et al., 2013). Researchers have documented that fathers want to care for their children. They want a more supportive role in their children's lives (DeGarmo, 2010; Shreffler et al., 2011). Schools have more willing dads than ever to work with. But what to do with them? Even with more fathers being the primary caregivers, their presence in schools remains spotty. This is partially due to indifferent outreach. Here or there, dads may be invited to participate in "Walk Your Child to School Day," a "Dads and Donuts" event, or a "Take Your Father to School Day." But what about all the other days? What about the other school events?

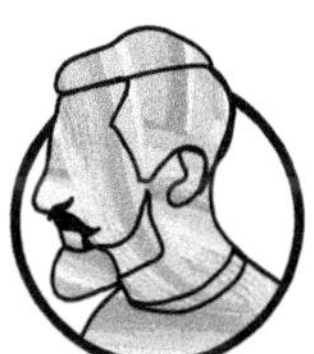

JOHN

"My dad worked most of the day. He would leave early and drop me off at school around 6:30 or 7:00 a.m. and would not come home until the evening, around 7:00. He worked an hour away, so my mom took the lead on my education. But at the same time, my dad would always, kind of before dropping us off every day, say, "Hey, let me know if you need help in any subject" or what not. When he would get home, he would kind of check in, make sure our homework and projects were done, see if we needed help studying in any specific subjects or anything like that. If there was a parent-teacher conference, it was usually my mom in there, but it was good to know that they were on the same page and continually being there and showing support. As my two sons grow up, and they get into the more academic stuff, I want to be there for them. Then it carries over to the guys I coach and mentor now, too."

Paternal Versus Maternal Interactions

Research shows that fathers interact with their children differently than mothers (Murphy, 2016). Their interactions aren't better or worse; they're just different. For example, fathers are more likely than mothers to engage their children in activities like playing catch, riding bikes, or going swimming—physical play that is critical to their development (Amodia-Bidakowska et al., 2020). These activities help lay the groundwork for children's social and emotional skills. Engaging in physical activity with their fathers can increase oxytocin in children, which helps reduce stress and anxiety by promoting trust and connection with others and is highest when children are engaged in safe, enjoyable activities (Machin, 2019).

Fathers also tend to discipline children differently than mothers do, sometimes in ways that can help kids learn healthy ways to manage frustration. For example, fathers are more likely than mothers to use humor and teasing to redirect behavior. They also tend to emphasize different vocabulary and ideas when reading aloud to their children, often adding sounds or acting out parts instead of just sitting and reading. This kind of playfulness has been shown to boost children's vocabulary skills in prekindergarten, while the effect of mothers' playfulness is more likely to help children develop emotional regulation skills (Cabrera et al., 2017). Dads are just as likely as moms to say that parenting is extremely important to their identity. Approximately 58 percent of mothers and 57 percent of fathers consider parenting to be extremely important to them. Like moms, many dads also seem to appreciate the benefits of parenthood: 54 percent reported that parenting is rewarding all the time, as did 52 percent of moms (Pew Research Center, 2015).

Healing Father Wounds

The men we interviewed had a lot to say about what it felt like to grow up without a present dad, and how it affected their outlook, behavior, and sense of security. Here's just a sampling:

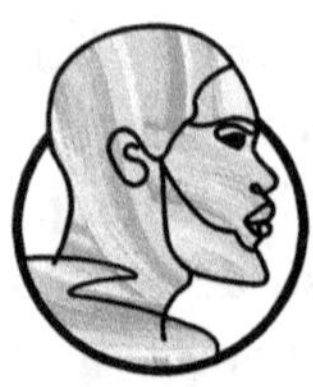

SAMUEL

"You find ways to make it. I have tried to change that mentality—that *it's cool; I don't need a father* mentality—because I was like that. You know, *I don't need him.* It is trauma that is being masked. . . . It makes you feel like, *Why me? What did I do?*"

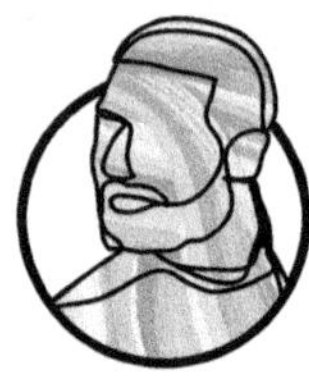

DAVID

"I agree that it is a trauma, and it can mess up your mental. As a kid, sometimes you just feel like, why didn't my dad want to be there? Was it me?"

PETER

"It's definitely a trauma, not having a father in your life to help guide you, because it's like you are guessing every step of the way."

These words capture the experience of countless students walking school hallways today. They are suffering from "father wounds"—the emotional and psychological damage linked to growing up without a father or without the right kind of father.

As Samuel, David, and Peter stated, and as the research confirms, children from fatherless homes are often traumatized by this absence. "It can mess up your mental," as David said. In *Spit'N Anger,* Kenneth Braswell's 2014 documentary about fatherlessness, inspirational speaker and life coach Iyanla Vanzant puts it this way:

> The anger the children feel about the absence of their father is real. We become angry when we don't get the love we think we deserve. Right beneath the anger is the hurt. The hurt is

> what makes children feel vulnerable. But instead of feeling [the hurt], they stay stuck in the anger. This is because they don't have the language or skills to express what they are feeling so the anger expands.

When we asked the men we interviewed to try to put their experiences of fatherlessness into words and describe how it affects them still, they said things like this:

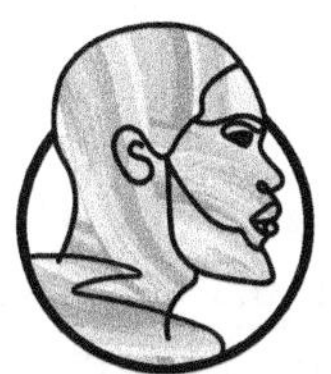

SAMUEL

"Not having a father is a constant. It can be a constant in a negative way, if you allow it to be. . . . I feel the trauma a lot in little things—when I am taking my daughter to get her shots, or I am making her food, or she's throwing up and I am making sure that she's OK, or I'm doing laundry. Like, these little things sometimes can be a trigger. . . . I'll be honest: in the early stages of my fatherhood little things like this, things *I* didn't have—it made me want to walk away. But I realized that I want to break that cycle. It's still a sensitive topic with me; however, it gets better when you have these types of conversations and you are vulnerable. It takes time."

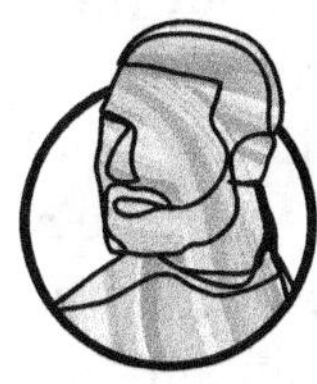

DAVID

"This idea of the absence of your father being a trauma is what I just sat with for the last five minutes. It certainly is. In fact, the impending birth of my son is bringing up new feelings about fatherhood that I thought I was cool on, right? Now I have a son on the way, and it's like *wooo*. The first thing that I have been hovering on is I wish I had been anticipated the way I am anticipating him. When you talk about the trauma and all of that stuff, it's literally the *wanting* [what you didn't have] that gets you."

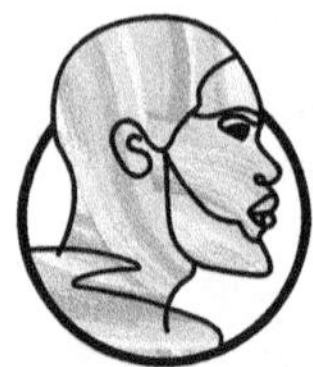

SAMUEL

"You've got to determine how you can move forward so that your children don't feel those traumas that we experienced."

The impact of fatherlessness is broader than we can address in this book. Fatherlessness doesn't just wound children; it wounds *families,* and the damage can extend over generations.

The Engaged Father

If there is a remedy, it's engagement. When schools collaborate with fathers as active participants in their children's education, benefits to students can include higher grades, better attendance and behavior, and improved social-emotional skills. In short, the research shows that schools' efforts to engage dads are likely worth it, given the great rewards that follow.

When fathers are engaged, there is a level of accountability that develops between them and their children. The dads we interviewed described accountability as checking in regularly with their children to make sure they are well. An accountable father, they said, asks his children about their school experiences. He shows concern about the learning environment. The engaged father has conversations about his children's friends and social activities to make sure they are making good choices. He knows the school activities and clubs they are involved in and inquires how he can support them in these endeavors. He makes sure his children have the necessary school supplies to participate in classes and complete special projects.

The men we interviewed who did not grow up with their fathers shared how much they valued the relationships they developed with their friends' dads. They were grateful that when their friends' fathers checked in on their own kids—asking about what they were learning, their homework, their grades—the friends' fathers checked in on them, too. They also shared how important coaches were in their lives and how for many of them, the coach took on that same father or mentor role by checking in on them regularly and holding them accountable. For these fatherless boys, the mere presence of their friends' dads and their coaches at school events led them to stand taller and be on their best behavior. The gift of their presence was more valuable than any tangible gift could be. As Samuel said, "Being present is better than presents."

THOMAS

"My dad was super hands-on. Just seeing him walking through the school let me know to act right. [He was] on a first-name basis with the teachers. They knew he was checking in, not waiting for the progress reports, not waiting until it's too late. He was there at parent-teacher conferences, he even started working at my school. I don't know if I would go to that extent, but I will definitely be present."

What Is the Difference Between Fathers and Dads?

In this book, we use the terms *father* and *dad.* Both refer to a male parent, but they carry distinct emotional and relational meanings. While every dad is a father, not every father fulfills the role of a dad. The difference lies in the depth of connection, presence, and emotional involvement. A *father* is a biological male or legal male parent, but a *dad* is a nurturing, supportive figure who actively participates in a child's life.

A *father* is defined by genetics, but a *dad* is defined by closeness, love, and presence. A *father* can provide financial support either voluntarily or legally, but a *dad* provides consistent care because this is his desire, not his obligation. To summarize, a father gives life, but a dad gives love. The father's role begins with creation; the dad's role continues through connection. One is a title by birth, the other a bond built through time, presence, and care. That's the dad difference. And when it's factored into the equation of schooling, the results are powerful.

CHAPTER

Getting Started with Father Engagement

Given the research findings we have just covered, interviews we've conducted, and our own experience of being in schools and around kids, we know that fathers are important to the overall social, emotional, and physical development of children. We know that their presence or absence can make a tremendous difference. We know, too, that dads care. In all our interviews with fathers, they stressed that they want to be involved in their children's education. We have also personally experienced the greater sense of staff well-being you'll find in schools where fathers are actively engaged in consistent, meaningful ways. As author Robyn Jackson (2024) puts it, "We don't have to be taught as much as we must be reminded [what to do] to be successful. We don't really need to know anything new as much as we need to constantly practice what we already know to be true."

When it comes to engaging fathers, the first moves matter tremendously. Maintaining carefully designed processes and systems that not only engage fathers but *keep them* engaged requires effort and commitment, especially in the beginning.

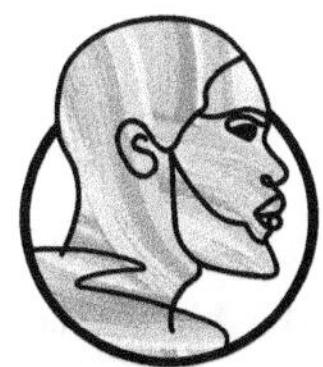

SAMUEL

"The time is now. We need action now."

Taking Stock

The first step in developing an effective father engagement program is to assess the current state of parental involvement at a school (Ferguson, 2005). You need information about specific areas of need, which requires you to get perspectives from key groups of stakeholders.

There's no need for complicated logistics; in fact, it's best to keep things simple and designate a single member of the school leadership team to oversee this process. This administrator will be responsible for ensuring confidentiality in both the outreach and the handling of stakeholder responses.

Find Out What Staff Think

The first step is to take stock of your school's current parent engagement efforts from the inside—by surveying staff. We recommend that all staff complete the questionnaire in Figure 2.1 before they leave for the summer; this way, administrators have a chance to review the data generated to purposefully plan engagement initiatives for the first semester of a new school year.

We recommend reissuing the same questionnaire at the end of the quarter or semester to evaluate how initiatives are working and to make any needed adjustments. We suggest to do it once more at the end of the school year. Examining the data at these various evaluation points is a good way to assess the effectiveness of your ongoing engagement efforts and support the planning of new initiatives for the upcoming year.

Ask Fathers Specifically

Few schools ask fathers, specifically, about the best way to communicate with them or what will motivate them to partner with schools. But schools desperately need fathers' first-person perspectives to make informed decisions, improve services, enhance fathers' experiences at school events, and build stronger relationships between them.

You can use the questionnaire in Figure 2.2 to find out how students' fathers prefer to engage with the school. Proactively inviting fathers to provide input in this way helps to cultivate their trust. Try giving this survey to fathers at Parents Night, when they drop off their children at school, or even while they're waiting in the carpool lane.

FIGURE 2.1

Parental Engagement Questionnaire for School Staff

Completed by: ________________________ Date: ____________

1. How are we currently engaging parents?
2. What do we purposefully do that invites parents to be active participants in our school?
3. How do we communicate our need for parents' involvement? (e.g., newsletter, email, phone)
4. What are the demographics of parents who usually attend our school events?
5. What motivates the parents who attend events at our school to do so?
6. Whose voices are missing from school meetings and events?
7. Do fathers feel welcome in our school? What evidence shows us that they do or do not?
8. How often do fathers attend events at our school other than parents night and sporting events?
9. Specifically, what have we done to purposefully invite fathers to engage with our school?
10. How do we communicate students' academic success or concerns to fathers?
11. Are there fathers of students at school who are not listed on the contact form? If so, how do we communicate with them?
12. Do fathers have opportunities to collaborate on improving student achievement? If so, in what ways?
13. Other than administrators, how often do school staff members meet with dads?
14. What are three goals we hope to meet by engaging fathers this year?

FIGURE 2.2

Parental Engagement Questionnaire for Fathers

Completed by: ______________________ Date: __________

Child(ren)'s name(s) and grade(s): ______________________

Relationship (e.g., father, stepfather, grandfather): ______________

Contact information (email and/or phone): ______________________

1. How are you involved in your child(ren)'s school(s)?
2. How would you like to be involved?
3. How often do you receive direct communications from your child(ren)'s school?
4. How would you like to receive communications from the school (e.g., calls, texts, emails), and how often?
5. How often have you met either virtually or face-to-face with school staff about your child(ren)?
6. Do you feel welcomed at your child(ren)'s school?
7. Is your child(ren)'s schoolwork shared with you? If so, when and by whom?
8. Have you had opportunities to collaborate with the school on improving student achievement? If yes, in what ways?
9. Are you listed on the parent contact information form? Did you share your phone number and/or email address?
10. How would you recommend getting more fathers involved in the school?
11. What specific topics would you like the school to address?
12. What are the best days and times for you to volunteer at school?

Survey the PTA

Finally, the questionnaire in Figure 2.3 is designed to solicit information from the school's parent–teacher association (PTA), which is typically run by mothers and has low rates of father participation. When the National PTA (2021) embarked on an effort to promote more inclusion, by partnering with the Center for Family Engagement to "reimagine family engagement practices and policies for greater effectiveness," they found that too many school-based PTAs failed to identify the lack of father participation as a handicap. To prevent this, a survey capturing the actual data can be a wake-up call—a galvanizing push to bring in more dads. The results can inform revisions to recruitment efforts and event planning and even spur the development of new PTA roles for fathers.

You can use these questionnaires as they are or adjust them and distribute them to your school leadership team, front office staff, guidance counselors, and others to learn more about how involved fathers are in your school. They can even be reworked to be interactive online documents.

As mentioned earlier, we recommend using all three questionnaires in a formative way: surveying multiple times during the school year and comparing the results to gauge the efficacy of your engagement efforts. This means you might use these questionnaires both to kick-start conversations about engaging fathers in their children's education and then to make them part of an ongoing process of reflection, revision, and reengagement.

"Actions speak louder than words," writes Dwayne Chism in his book *Leading Your School Toward Equity*. Schools, he adds, must "commit to taking the necessary actions to provide an environment that remains in tune with the experiences of those who come from various backgrounds and conditions. You [the administrator] are the leading factor in

FIGURE 2.3

Father Engagement Questionnaire for the PTA

Completed by: ______________________ Date: ____________

1. Are fathers and/or male guardians from varied backgrounds represented in the PTA?
2. Who is missing at PTA meetings? Why? If you don't know, how can you find out?
3. Do you actively cultivate interest among fathers and/or male guardians to serve in the PTA? If so, how?
4. What days and times are meetings held, and where?
5. What PTA activities do fathers participate in the most?
6. How often do you communicate PTA events specifically to fathers?
7. Roughly what percentage of fathers and/or male guardians in your community would you estimate attends school events?
8. Does the PTA plan any events specifically geared toward engaging fathers and/or male guardians?
9. What tool(s) are you using to measure your success with engaging fathers and/or male guardians?
10. What concerns, challenges, or roadblocks have you faced trying to get fathers and/or male guardians more involved in school?
11. What are some potential benefits of having a more fully engaged community of fathers and/or male guardians in the PTA?
12. What are your next steps? Who will take them and when, and how will you measure success?

creating and sustaining environmental change. The commitment starts with you" (p. 14).

When reviewing the parental presence in your school, consider also whether the school has a gender bias. Are programs, communications, and opportunities geared toward one gender rather than both? Do men teach across subjects at the school or just physical education or science classes? Are there any male cafeteria workers or school nurses in the school? Have there ever been? What norms and values does your reality reflect? Are they aligned with your ideals? What would it look like to bring reality and ideals closer together?

Decoding the Data

Once you've collected data on father engagement, use that information strategically to strengthen relationships, improve participation, and guide decision making. You want to use data to inform smarter action—not just gather it for documentation.

First thing you can do is look for trends. For example, when examining participation patterns, such as which events or programs attract the most fathers, ask yourself if the data reveal demographic insights or barriers to engagement. You can use the data to inform future plans, to promote future plans, and to testify to the effectiveness of your plans. If you find that a significant number of dads in the community work shifts, for example, adjust event times accordingly. Explain this adjustment in a school newsletter. Track the resulting shifts in dad participation and celebrate successes in newsletters down the line.

Deborah recalls collecting father engagement data and academic data and publicizing the results to show a correlation between increased numbers of fathers participating in school programs and activities and a rise in student success. Her school incorporated this data in its school improvement plans and expanded father partnership to the community's feeder schools.

By analyzing, applying, and sharing father engagement data, schools can create a cycle of continuous improvement that strengthens family partnerships and supports student success. Use questionnaire responses to identify the areas where gender inclusion can be improved. Use them to guide staff discussions and professional development activities aimed at promoting more equitable parent engagement. Use them to figure out how your parent programs are currently functioning, what constructive roles fathers could be playing, and what kinds of opportunities to offer them.

To form a successful partnership with fathers, thinking through what you really need from them and writing it out concisely will help you choose engagement strategies specific to your school's needs and, thus, ones more likely to appeal to your students' dads.

For example, at one school where Deborah worked, kids were coming to school but skipping class. She and her staff decided to tell the dads they were reaching out to that they needed help brainstorming solutions to the school's internal truancy problem. As it turned out, brainstorming wasn't necessary. As soon as dads started coming to the school regularly and were present in our school for several hours during the day, internal truancy evaporated. The dads' presence alone was enough to spur students to go to class.

What Counts as Constructive Engagement?

Effective parental involvement programs allow parents multiple ways to participate, are long-lasting, and are well organized. Another essential ingredient is the right kind of leadership. To set up the distributed, participatory structure that sustains a school–parent partnership, the initial leadership needs to be decisive. As Ferguson (2005) puts it, "Schools, families, and communities need strong leadership [in order] to shift away from the traditional models of involvement in which school personnel dominate the interactions" (p. 20).

When thinking of what your school is currently doing to engage parents and where you might be falling short, it's helpful to consider the five functions of parent engagement programs identified by Wirtz and Schumacher (2003):

1. To share information with parents and families
2. To welcome parents and families
3. To involve parents and families in school-based programs
4. To support learning at home
5. To work with the community

The first function on this list—to share information—is carried out by sending home newsletters, posting announcements on shared bulletin boards, and preparing and distributing activity calendars. What are you currently doing on this front? How confident are you that information your school shares is reaching dads, specifically? How could you investigate this further?

The next two functions of parent engagement programs—to welcome parents and families and to involve them in programs—consider the way parents are received and treated when they interact with school personnel, including their experiences volunteering their time and expertise. What do you currently do to make all parents and families feel like members of your school community, part of a mutually beneficial relationship? How might these efforts be resonating with dads?

The next function Wirtz and Schumacher identify—to support learning at home—includes the guidance schools offer parents on basic homework assistance and additional activities (like skills practice) that can support student learning.

Is this something you're currently doing? How are you going about it? What evidence do you have that this guidance is reaching dads and that they are acting on it?

The fifth function—to work with the community—includes the collaboration among school, parents, and the larger community to sponsor events or programs. What activities does your school offer that rely on parent and community cooperation? How many fathers are active in these efforts? What roles do they play? Are there any community activities that tend to draw dads that the school might partner with, such as a reading event or a book exchange hosted by a local barbershop or recreational sports league?

Now take a step back and consider fathers' roles overall. Ask yourself: Are the dads in your school truly *engaged*, or are they only nominally *involved?* Why or why not? And how does your school communicate to fathers that their *engagement* is what you want and need?

Asking Versus Inviting

Although teachers are the educators most likely to have direct contact with parents, communication to fathers should be a united front, led by the administration. They can do a lot to encourage parental involvement by being visible during parent meetings, motivating and encouraging staff to improve home–school communication, and leading parent engagement activities (Epstein & Sanders, 2006; Shartrand et al., 1997). School leaders set the climate of the school, which influences whether there are positive relationships among parents, and set the tone for positive communication that's built not on *asking* but on *inviting.*

What's the difference between an ask and an invitation? An *ask* is meant to get a simple yes-or-no answer. Because it generally serves a practical purpose, an ask also tends to have transactional tone, aimed at achieving a specific objective rather than fostering conversation: "Can you come to the next parent meeting?" In contrast, an *invitation* seeks to open a dialogue and create a connection. Its tone is relational and inclusive; it aims to encourage collaboration and indicates interest in the other person's opinions: "We'd really value your perspective at our next parent meeting and would love you to be there to contribute to the conversation." Note that neither asks nor invitations need to be phrased as questions. "Our students have been working hard on their special science projects, and they would love to share them with you this Thursday" is an invite. Contrast its tone and aims with an equivalent ask: "Can you please come out Thursday to see the science projects?" For a third example of invitation, consider "We're hosting an Open House next Friday morning. Join us from 8:00 to 8:30 for coffee and conversation as we highlight the father's mentoring program and the difference it is making in our students lives." Do you see how this phrasing is likely to be more effective at building lasting connection and engagement than the ask "Friday is our Open House. Can you make it?" If asking perpetuates an "us versus them" paradigm, inviting presents a "we" opportunity (Mitchell, 2022). Or as Phillips (2023) puts it, "When you invite someone, you are forming a relationship" (para. 2).

Contacting Fathers

A school may or may not have an official policy on which parent to contact when there's a need to reach out, but ask any father you know, and they are likely to tell you that if their child gets sick, the school will typically call his or her mother first. When fathers are called in, it is usually for discipline problems or as a "last resort." Rarely are they called in for educational or fun activities. This oversight, which may seem innocuous, can result in fathers feeling unwelcome or out of place at their children's school. It can fuel the perception that dads are an afterthought. Some schools have alienated fathers so much that when they do reach out to them, the father's first response is "What has happened that is so bad that you are calling me?"

We have heard this a lot through our years as administrators, before we started intentionally reaching out to fathers. It reflects expectations about families: that the moms are the involved and interested ones and fathers "don't want to be bothered." Another factor is that school staff are primarily women and may feel more comfortable calling another woman instead of a man. Changing this mindset requires deliberate effort. Getting started with father engagement means doing father outreach and communication differently.

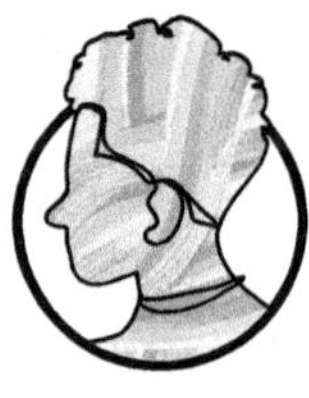

BENJAMIN

"Everyone has cellphones. You need us? Contact us. You need me to help get other fathers involved? Let's sit down and talk and plan this out. I want my kids to go to a school that wants me there."

When Deborah became an administrator, she didn't know that schools "weren't supposed" to call dads. So, she called them. Once she saw the results, she was hooked. It led to a formalized strategy she called "Phone Fathers First." The strategy was simple: school personnel with a reason to place a call home committed to calling students' fathers first, before calling the students' mothers.

About those results: If it was a "good news" call, the student usually came to school the next day beaming and excited. Why? Because Dad had made a big deal about something they had accomplished or achieved. If the call addressed a challenge, the student usually came to school upset but then changed their behavior. Phone Fathers First calls were win-win situations for Deborah's school. Yes, it was effective in improving behavior;

negative behaviors decreased by 80 percent for all students and stayed at this lower level for as long as the strategy was in place. But the simple recognition of the father's parenting role was also a practical way to plant seeds for a partnership. When Deborah and her team started recruiting dads for their growing father engagement program, these men were already comfortable communicating with the school. There was an established relationship.

Chacko has found that reaching out to fathers first and talking with them directly—whether the subject is a child's behavior or learning progress or the overall classroom dynamic—builds trust with dads and demonstrates the school's view that dads' input and teamwork are valued. It's true that male staff may have an easier time with "direct dad contact" at the start; the fathers appreciate being able to discuss concerns with someone they believe will more easily understand what they're going through. But simply defaulting to making fathers the first contact can be enough to broaden dads' sense of shared responsibility for what goes on in school and increase their support in a way that improves classroom management and student success.

Since 2007, both of us have implemented the Phone Fathers First strategy in different schools with similar results. In all cases, we shared the resulting data with staff and families, which had the effect of encouraging more fathers to provide the school with their contact information.

There are educators who think effective communication is any communication—send out regular emails or newsletters, and you're doing it right—but this is not the case (Valenzuela, 2024). Mass communications of that sort tend to be ignored due to something called *narcotizing dysfunction* (Lee, 2016). When there's too much undifferentiated messaging, people tune it out. Think about it: How many robocalls do you actually listen to? How many emails do you ignore or delete without reading? How closely do you read the newsletters you receive?

Do you scour each one for information that might potentially affect you, and then follow up?

In our experience, when inviting fathers to partner with your school, a direct approach is best—and try to keep it short. Even if there are many things your school could gain from fathers' presence and contributions, keep your message brief and focused when you first reach out. For example:

- Fathers, we need you!
- Students do well when mothers are involved in their education, but they excel when their fathers are involved.
- Dads! We looked at our data and noticed something was missing: you!
- Last fall, only 3 percent of all field trip chaperones were fathers. Help us change that.
- We can't spell *SUCCESS* without *U!*

Training Staff to Welcome and Work with Dads

Teachers and administrators need to build the knowledge and receive the tools necessary to actively engage fathers in their kids' education. We recommend consulting the following resources, which can help to guide home-grown professional development activities:

- *Let's Talk Back to School: Sample Questions Parents and Families Can Ask to Partner with Your Child's Teachers and School* (U.S. Department of Education, 2024). This handout has 20 questions parents can use during the school year when communicating with their children's school. The questions are divided into topics on how to partner for students' success, maintain ongoing communications, and work together for students' academic progress. Not only are these questions starting places for parents, but they can also be used at father engagement meetings to kick off meaningful conversations about issues that are important to dads and to schools.

- Building Partnerships with Families (Head Start, 2025). Often schools think they are doing well with parent engagement by hosting an annual open house or fall parent conferences. These are events, not engagement. The Building Partnerships with Families online course is a way for staff to enhance their understanding and practice of family engagement using strength-based attitudes, relationship-based practices, and reflective practices. It's designed to help a school move beyond surface involvement toward true engagement and build staff understanding of why doing so will improve school outcomes.
- "Building Strong Partnerships: 10 Effective Strategies for Teachers to Engage Parents and Guardians" (Cube, 2025). The anonymous author of this blog post is a principal who has seen firsthand how strong partnerships between schools and parents can boost student success. His suggestions are timely and practical. They can be implemented by a private or public school that's large or small, urban or rural.
- *60 Parent Engagement Ideas to Boost School Improvement* (Wallace, 2024). We recommend this resource because it includes both the usual suggestions and more niche ideas, such as how to build relationships with parents when there are significant practical barriers. It also distinguishes itself by including parental engagement ideas for middle and high schools.

Staff may also need time to express their thoughts and discuss the mechanics of their involvement. For some, engaging fathers may conjure unpleasant memories from their own childhoods; they may need to discuss this one-on-one with an administrator. Remind staff that fathers are their partners in education.

Back-Mapping for Engagement

We encourage school leaders to "back-map" plans for father engagement: envision where you want your program to be by the end of the school year, semester, quarter and then build a strategic plan to keep moving, step by step, toward it. What are the outcomes you want to see for your school, your students, and their dads? In your planning team, clarify what successful father engagement looks like (e.g., fathers feeling welcomed, participating regularly, and contributing to school life), and then work backward to determine what kinds of communications, invitations, relationship-building moments, and scheduling decisions are needed to move toward that vision.

As a practical first step forward, try aligning father-focused activities with existing school events, such as concerts, plays, athletic contests, or family nights. Because many families are already on campus for these activities, schools do not need to rely on an entirely separate evening or expect fathers to make an additional trip. A father who has come to watch a basketball game, for instance, may pass a display about an upcoming engagement opportunity or stop by a table to connect with a staff member. This approach lowers barriers, builds familiarity, and helps fathers transition naturally from being occasional visitors to active partners in school life.

If you know there is a regular event that normally draws a large crowd, make that a time for a father engagement meeting or activity. See how many dads show up. Compare the turnout to previous years or to other dad-focused events. You can also use the "co-scheduled" events to advertise your father engagement program. Fathers attending a football game may see signs up about a fathers' meeting and stop by out of curiosity. Here are a few tips:

- Set up a table in the lobby or in an area that parents must walk by on their way to the headline school event.
- Post signs and posters pointing dads to the table and inviting them to stop in.
- Assign your most welcoming staff members, especially any who are male, to greet fathers and call them over to the table.
- At the table, phrase your invitations for involvement in a way that makes it clear to fathers that this is an opportunity to support his child's school by helping the teachers and students.
- If fathers express interest in volunteering, get all their contact information right then. Make sure to get full names, email addresses, and cell phone numbers. Include a place on the form for dads to share information about their children—first name, last name, grade level—as well as days and times when the father is likely to be available. *Note:* Last name is important, especially if the child's and parent's names are different.

The Initial Fathers' Meeting

Once a number of fathers have expressed interest in volunteering, schedule a fathers' meeting within two weeks. Prior to the meeting, reach out by phone or email to other fathers with whom you have a positive relationship but who did not sign up and ask them to attend the meeting, too. Tell them that you are contacting them because you need someone you already know to help you, and their presence will make the other fathers feel more comfortable. Ask if there are any other fathers they know who might be interested; if they share any names, follow up with them on the same day.

Once you have set a date for an initial fathers' meeting, plan the agenda. The first meeting should be about establishing purpose; clearly state one or two school needs that fathers can help with—but no more than one or two, as you don't want to overwhelm them. Choose opportunities that are manageable and yield measurable results, such as helping to monitor hallways during the school day or chaperoning a field trip. Yes, it may look more like involvement than engagement, but involvement is a first step. It's something to build on.

Here are some additional recommendations that will help you plan and implement a successful first fathers' meeting, one that will be a solid foundation for more:

- **Document it all.** Make sure you have a note taker (a staff member or a volunteer dad) to take minutes and keep a record of which fathers will attend which events.
- **Introduce some possible engagement opportunities,** such as those shared in Chapter 4.
- **Ask fathers what activities interest them.** Activities that allow fathers to show off their skills, knowledge, and expertise (and help build students' skills, knowledge, and expertise) are always good choices because they generate positive feelings of pride and accomplishment in both the dads and their children. Fathers might talk about subjects they took in school that they use regularly in their current jobs, why, and how. They might teach a skill, such as how to use a new technology app during a science lesson or how to serve and volley in a physical education class, or they might help students who are struggling with calculator skills to practice them.
- **Encourage fathers to modify events based on the needs of your school and community.** For example,

instead of having a single Saturday school walking event where some students may not have transportation to attend, do a regular school mini-walk during each lunch period.

- **Ask fathers to verify their contact information and commit to at least one school event that quarter.** Get that commitment in writing, and before adjourning the meeting, review the action items everyone has committed to, when they'll do it, and how they'll go about it.
- **Always have a "next time."** Engagement is never a "one-and-done" activity; it's an ongoing process. Plan the date and time for the next fathers' meeting in collaboration with the dads before the conclusion of the current meeting.

Within 48 hours of the meeting, follow up with a brief email sharing notes from the meeting and the list of who volunteered to do what. You may also broadcast the meeting to the community via newsletter or mass phone call, letting them know that fathers are coming together to collaborate with the school on actionable school improvement and student achievement goals. We found that doing this generated more interest from fathers. In your message, make sure to invite any interested fathers to take part and include contact information.

Father Engagement in Action

This is Deborah writing. Educators know the best plans begin with the end in mind. It's about identifying the desired outcomes and working backwards to figure out how to achieve them. So, before we conclude this "getting started" chapter, we want to share an example of the kind of positive, authentic, and transformational father engagement you're working toward, and of the kind of complicated context you may be working within.

Deborah's Experience with the Fathers' Circle

The father engagement efforts I want to hold up for examination are those I spearheaded myself in collaboration with colleagues and the dads at our Maryland middle school.

We were halfway into the second quarter of the school year when the Community Four Team, consisting of 6th–8th grade teachers, came together to discuss student achievement data. One student was having difficulty in every subject, and the teachers had no idea how to help him. "There's nothing else we can do," one of them said. "We've tried every strategy and intervention known to man!"

Although I was a new administrator in a new school, I had worked with this student and was not ready to throw in the towel. "What about calling his dad and talking to him about what is going on?" I asked.

Ours was a majority white school. All the teachers in this meeting were white. They looked skeptical. "He doesn't have a dad," said one. "Black kids don't have fathers, at least not at home."

I was stunned by this comment and by the false assumptions behind it. For one thing, I am a Black woman who grew up with my father. I also knew that the majority of the Black students at our school did, in fact, have fathers in their homes, and this included the student we were talking about. I shared this information with the teachers, and what happened next changed my career trajectory.

One teacher challenged me to prove that fathers could be involved in their children's education. We were starting parent conferences in a week, and this teacher challenged me to invite fathers to attend. "We *never* get Black fathers to show up for conferences," she said. "Mothers, yes; fathers, no. Go ahead and invite them, but I bet not one will show."

My anger was rising. "I will!" I said and left the meeting, worried that if I stayed, I might say something that would forever ruin my relationship with these teachers.

Once I got my feelings in check, I prayed. "What should I do?" I asked. "Do what she said," responded my spirit. "Invite fathers to the conferences." The problem was, there were too many fathers for me to personally invite to the conferences, which were one week away. The school had approximately 1,300 students. It was divided into four quads, and my quad had more than 300 students. So, I divided the work up among myself, team leaders, and the school secretaries. We called every student's father—regardless of the student's race, culture, and academic standing—and extended a personal conference invitation. And every single student, including every Black student on my team, had a father show up, whether it was a biological dad, a stepfather, or another adult male living at home. I cried when I saw the stream of fathers, especially the fathers of our Black students, coming into our school.

Following the parent conferences, staff immediately noticed a change in students' behavior. Discipline issues for *all* students dropped by 70 percent over the next week. This was a drastic improvement that none of us had anticipated. Everyone was surprised—even me. We had record numbers of students completing their homework. The number of Black students achieving honor roll status increased by 12 percent that quarter.

Though the results held steady for the rest of the quarter, they were based on a single initiative, so we were skeptical that they would last. To keep up the momentum, I started a new group—the Fathers' Circle—composed of men who regularly met at the school and attended all school functions. Every month, between 40 and 50 fathers attended these meetings. When we began to combine them with our Family Math and Reading Nights and with PTA meetings, the numbers rose to over 100. Most of the students at the school were neither

Black nor Latino, but most of the fathers at these affairs were. However, once the word got out that Black and Latino men were the majority at all meetings and school events, white and Asian fathers quickly joined in. It was heartwarming to see dads coming together for their children.

One of the greatest accomplishments of the Fathers' Circle was securing a $10,000 grant from America Online to take all 8th graders on college visits. Many of these students didn't even know what a college campus looked like. For these visits, we asked that only fathers attend as chaperones. This was the first time many of them had visited a college campus, too. A few cried and said that if they'd had a similar experience in middle school, they were positive their lives would have turned out better. The trips took place in the fall, when the campuses in Maryland are at their most inviting. Some fathers were surprised at the atmosphere: how students casually walked to classes or sat and chatted in the student halls. Many dads told us they didn't know so many Black and Latino students attended college. The Fathers' Circle enabled fathers as a group to share in both their children's joys and struggles as students and their own joys and struggles as dads. Today, when I see dads or students who participated in Fathers' Circle events, we all share how it felt to be a part of something so special.

I am tremendously proud of all it's achieved. I am confident you can get similar results in your school, with your students and their dads.

A Critical Moment of Connection for Chacko

This is Chacko with some thoughts to add. A realization that changed everything for me was that fathers generally aren't disengaged from their child's school because they don't care; they're disengaged because they never felt like they were invited to engage. Like many schools, mine had an annual evening gathering where parents could meet teachers, learn about expectations, and start the year as partners in their kids' education. At the end of the night, each child's parents were handed a volunteer form to fill out telling the school how they wanted to be involved. Usually, this form ended up with the moms. They were the ones who most often filled it out, sent it back, and eventually became the regular volunteers in our classrooms.

One year, I decided to try something different. Instead of giving out a single volunteer form per family, I made sure to give a form to all parents, moms and dads. It was a small thing, but it sent a big message: *You're both welcome here. You're both needed here.*

In the days that followed, the returned forms started telling a new story. Fathers began signing up—a lot of fathers! They volunteered to help during math, reading, and science classes. Some signed up to read with small groups of students. Others offered to help with hands-on projects, experiments, and problem solving.

We felt the impact right away. Having fathers in the classroom really changed the vibe. When students saw their dads arriving to lend a hand, they were so excited! Kids who usually seemed shy or distracted suddenly leaned in with fresh enthusiasm. There was a real sense of pride when a father came in to volunteer. Kids had evidence that learning was important to everyone—not just to teachers and moms but to dads, too.

In a school mostly run by women, having male role models added a whole new layer to the learning experience. Dads read stories with such expression and humor, helped students tackle tricky math problems, and joined in science experiments with curiosity and patience. Their involvement really showed that learning is for everyone and school is something we all take part in together.

Looking back, it's clear that the most important thing wasn't the volunteer form itself but the invitation it represented. By putting the form in fathers' hands, we showed them they belonged and that we wanted them to participate. We went from thinking they might join in to actively inviting them. That little gesture told fathers we wanted them to be valued partners in their children's education. Their response told us dads were ready to jump in; they just needed to know that they were wanted.

This lesson keeps shaping how I think about schools, families, and the community. When teachers create space for dads to participate, the benefits spread out—to classrooms, to families, and most importantly, to kids who really shine when they see both parents actively involved in their learning.

Other Program Examples

Here are a few more exemplars of what's possible in father engagement programs, beginning with Fathers Read 365 (fathersread365.org), a nonprofit organization run by dads Akeiff Staples and Brent Johnstone. The group distributes books to schoolchildren in Philadelphia and organizes literacy- and engagement-boosting father read-alouds in daycares and other settings. Their group also aims to help adults who struggle with reading comprehension. Programs like Fathers Read 365 can be replicated everywhere.

Another good example is Dads on Duty. A high school in Louisiana had so much violence on campus that a group of fathers decided to step in and do something. Note that the school did not reach out to them; the *fathers* stepped in on their own to start Dads on Duty. They went to their children's high school every day and were a presence in the halls. The violence stopped immediately (Fanning, 2022)

This is a reminder of how powerful a dad's mere presence can be. Their engagement can be transformational. Remembering this can sustain you through the challenges you will inevitably face, which we'll look at next.

CHAPTER

Overcoming Obstacles to Engagement

You had everything in place. Communications went out to hundreds. You set an agenda that was specifically designed to engage fathers. You sent reminders. Many fathers RSVPed, but only 10 showed up.

If you are having difficulty getting fathers to show up for engagement initiatives, don't stress. Many factors can influence parents' attendance at school functions, and most of those factors are outside your control. It's fine to start small and focus on building your program. If you get a lot of participation immediately, rejoice! You are a unicorn. But if only a few fathers respond at first, remember that this is the norm.

Both *who* is issuing the invitation to father engagement and *what* you're asking of fathers is very important, especially in the beginning. Experiment with switching the messenger and ask one or more of your school's engaged fathers to take over the outreach. Dad-to-dad communication seems to carry extra weight.

"A Few Good Men"

When Deborah's school started the Fathers' Circle, the low participation rates were disappointing. But it turns out that a few good men can be all you need.

Students noticed the handful of fathers who started showing up in the building. They observed them in the halls, during classes, in the cafeteria, and at dismissal. Without saying much beyond greeting students and giving a few words of encouragement ("Make today count!" "We believe in you!"), these dads made an incredible impression. Curious students who asked them why they were there got honest responses: "To help you learn and enable the staff to teach in a welcoming environment."

The presence of fathers made students feel special, and the impact on the fathers was similar. Students told their fathers, grandfathers, uncles, and other significant adult male figures in their lives about the dads in the building and asked them to participate. The fathers told other fathers about what they were doing and, more important, how it felt to be back in a school building, interacting with students. They told the other fathers how great it felt to be making a difference for their children and the school community.

Some students actually asked the school to contact their father and invite him to participate. If these direct overtures weren't successful, Deborah went to a Fathers' Circle member—one who was excited about his experience—and asked him to place a follow-up call and share his point of view as to why participation was important. "Just come once," this one good man urged. "Just come for an hour or two. If you don't want to continue, you won't be contacted again." This worked every time. Once the men got to the school and saw the comraderie between the dads, they were hooked. This, in conjunction with the positive interactions with students, kept them coming back. If you just get dads in the building, you're halfway there.

Every journey starts with a first step. At the outset, stress that the school is looking for fathers to show up for an orientation: a short meeting that will give them idea of what dad engagement is all about—what it can do for them, and what it can do for their children. Clarify that fathers who attend this meeting and decide afterward that they *don't* want to forge closer ties with the school will be removed from the outreach list for the remainder of the school year. Keep this promise. It will not hamper your efforts, because the pull of fellowship is so effective.

This is important, too: when fathers do show up, let them do their thing. By that, we mean explain their role or assignment, then resist the urge to micromanage. Relinquishing control can be difficult for some staff as well as for some active-volunteer moms, who naturally want to jump in to help. We always advise these seasoned volunteers to hang back. One sure way to run off newly involved fathers is to ask them to do something and then have someone else rush in and take over before they get through it.

You may have tried the usual outreach methods, and you may even have had students ask you to contact their fathers and invite them to participate. If you've done this and fathers are still reluctant to engage, don't give up. In this chapter, we'll cover a variety of ways to successfully navigate common obstacles to father engagement and sustain thriving partnerships with students' dads.

Scheduling Conflicts

Fathers who live at home with their children tend to spend the most time with them on the weekends (Yeung, 2001). It makes sense, then, try to plan events like community fairs, concerts, or performances on Saturdays or Sundays rather than on weekday evenings. When schools schedule all events during a standard time window, typically during the workday or from 7:00 p.m. to 9:00 p.m. Monday through Friday, dads who have non-traditional working hours can find themselves locked out.

Flexible options—early-morning breakfast events, evening activities, or weekend events—offer more opportunities for fathers to participate. Such small scheduling tweaks have a clear message: all fathers' time, voices, and presence are important in building a positive school culture. It is also important for schools to determine what times of the day are optimal for parental participation; fathers need choices that suit their schedules. For example, instead of asking dads to spend an entire day volunteering at school, consider creating shifts that they can sign up for (e.g., greeting students and staff in the first hour of school, talking to students in the cafeteria at lunchtime). Most important of all, though, is to explicitly invite fathers to donate their time and presence and explain what help is needed, in what form, and for how long. The more details schools provide, the more likely it is that fathers will pitch in.

As educators, we found that fathers did not feel the school was bothering them when reaching out about their children's education, no matter how busy they were with work. They wanted to contribute however they could to their children's well-being. Offering frequent and varied opportunities for engagement increases the number of fathers who can participate, and a distributed approach like this creates a strong and adaptable program—a better bet than relying on just one or two major events to bring in the dads. Ongoing and diverse opportunities is a way to appeal to and engage fathers who have a wide range of skills, schedules, and interests.

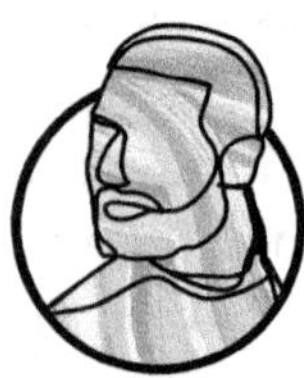

DAVID

"My generation is taking to this fatherhood thing. Everybody in my sphere, whether married or not, is putting in the work. Please amplify this. It's amazing."

One key is to share dates well in advance. We often had fathers take a day or two off work so they could volunteer during the school day; they just needed enough time to give their job notice. In fact, we even heard from several fathers' employers asking how *they* could get a fathers' program going at their children's schools!

Lack of Transportation

Some parents are willing and able to help at school but do not have a way to get there. It took Deborah's car breaking down for her to realize how impactful a lack of adequate transportation can be. By car, the trip to school took 10 minutes; by public transportation, it took almost 2 hours. And rideshare options like Uber and Lyft can be expensive.

To address transportation issues, ask fathers if they are available to pick up another dad who may need a ride to and from school on volunteering days. You can include this request on the form when signing them up to volunteer.

Deborah's school saw many friendships form because of these carpools. One father confided that he had never talked so much to his neighbor as he did when they rode to school functions together. Before, all they had done was wave to each other and maybe say "Hi" or "Good morning." During the rides to and from school, they realized they were both fans of the same football team (especially surprising, as it wasn't a local one). Soon they were regularly spotted standing together, talking about their day or about last night's game. Instead of just being neighbors, they became friends. These bonds also helped them to hold each other accountable for attending school events.

Negative Experiences with School

Many fathers resist engaging with their children's education because they had negative memories of their own time in school. Whether they did not do well academically, never felt like they fit in, or were on the receiving end of bullying or punishment, they still carry the trauma of their school experiences years later.

As fathers at Deborah's school continued to meet regularly, they became more comfortable talking to staff about negative experiences some had had when they were students. Once aware of the fathers' feelings, the meeting facilitator began devoting time during meetings for them to share their school stories. It was cathartic for the dads and informative for the staff.

Deborah's staff also used this opportunity to remind the fathers that this was a chance for them to change the narrative around schooling—for their children's sake and their own. Though wounded in the past, they could now become healers, using their negative experiences for good. During conversations with students as sports event volunteers, chaperones, mentors, and classroom assistants, some fathers were able to use their stories to help students avoid some of the hardships they themselves had experienced.

In 2008, Fathers' Circle co-chairs Patrick Gerdes and Morgan Thomas were honored as "Hometown Heroes" by WETA, a public television station in Greater Washington, DC. When asked how the program had affected him personally, Thomas talked about how much he learned from the other fathers in the group, who acted as mentors to him when it came to parenting his son. Gerdes said that the Fathers' Circle "gave me an opportunity to see the importance of the role we play as parents in setting expectations and shaping the environment" (Montgomery County Public Schools, 2007, p. 1). He went on to talk about the program's powerful impact within the school:

> The increased presence and involvement of fathers has been a key element in reducing conflicts and the suspension rates of boys, and most importantly it has reinforced the positive messages to our kids that their dads—as well as their moms—are committed to work with school staff to give them the best learning opportunities. The Fathers' Circle sought to live by the wise saying that 'it takes a village to raise a child' by bringing some male role models to the school to impact the environment for all kids, not just our own. (p. 7)

Isolation

Schools have a history of isolating fathers. Many dads feel that the school only calls them when there is a major problem, and often they are right.

To eliminate the obstacle that these negative feelings present, schools should start by acknowledging the problem. Develop a call-to-action statement. State a fact (e.g., "Dads! We need your help") and embed it in all messages to fathers, from emails to phone calls to posters.

Don't hesitate to enhance a call to action statement with data for father engagement research and from your school surveys, especially if your results show low attendance from dads at school events. For example: "Dads play a powerful role in shaping their children's success, yet only 10 percent of our fathers regularly attend school events. Let's raise that number and show our children that learning matters!" Call back to the overarching purpose that school engagement can help build regular participation that's not linked to any particular activity or event.

Another great way to ensure fathers don't feel isolated from school is to include stories about your engagement programs and opportunities in your newsletters. If you can, pack these stories with testimonials and direct quotes from your participating dads, which is something Deborah's school did. This will not only motivate them to keep coming back but also invigorate your staff, who are able to see that fathers are committed to their children's education, which generates both pride and appreciation in those students.

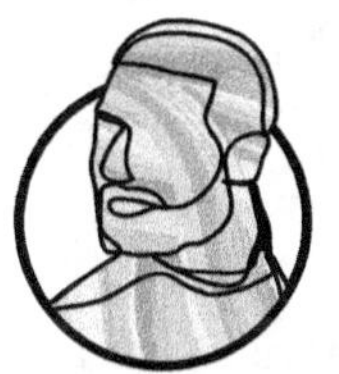

DAVID

"It all starts with having a great relationship with her teacher, really understanding that it's a partnership. I am very present in a way that I wish my dad had been. The 'check-in' when I was growing up was to make sure you weren't embarrassing them. The tone was more about making sure I was on the path to get what was needed, leading from a path of correction. It really didn't feel good. I am glad that we are speaking about the positives."

Incarceration

In most states, fathers who are incarcerated have the legal right to be included in virtual conferences and to receive school information, including report cards and disciplinary reports. Given the importance of parent–child relationships and the deep and often traumatic effect that a father's absence can have on a child, there has been a renewed focus on ensuring that schools reach out to incarcerated parents (Cramer et al., 2017).

Here are some ways to help ensure that fathers in prison remain engaged with their students' learning:

- Ask incarcerated fathers to record themselves reading their children's favorite books.
- Ask incarcerated fathers to record and share positive messages for students and include them with messages from other dads at the school.
- Invite incarcerated fathers to call into parent–teacher conferences.
- Encourage students to share photos of projects, awards, and activities with their incarcerated dads.
- Assign an administrator or counselor to serve as a contact person specifically for incarcerated fathers.
- Take events to the fathers. For example, in a 2012 TED Talk, Angela Patton shared how she planned and put on Virginia's first-ever father–daughter dance in a prison. As she put it, "Just because a father is locked in does not mean he should be locked out of his daughter's life."
- The National Responsible Fatherhood Clearinghouse suggests having children come up with fictional characters that the fathers then write about in stories, perhaps sharing a new chapter with their kids every month (Get Creative, Stay Connected, 2020).
- Ask incarcerated fathers to share art or keepsakes with their kids. For example, in one Missouri State prison, a group of fathers purchased plain white pillowcases from

the prison store. Using fabric markers, they created personalized pillowcases for their children and mailed them to them along with a handmade card (Get Creative, Stay Connected, 2020).

- If the mother is on good terms with the incarcerated father, ask if she'd be willing to help maintain his connection with their children. For example, one incarcerated father wanted to learn more about how his son was doing in school, so he sent the mother clasp envelopes pre-addressed to him in prison and asked her to send him any extra school papers she did not have room for or want to keep. Every few months, he received an envelope back full of his son's schoolwork, which he read carefully before writing a return letter praising his son and encouraging him to keep up the good work. As a result of this engagement, the father and son grew closer (Get Creative, Stay Connected, 2020).

Incarcerated dads face extraordinary obstacles keeping track of their children's development and activities, but they can surmount these with a little inspiration, some imagination, and plenty of encouragement from school staff.

Reluctance from School Leaders

But what if the reluctance comes from the school's administrators? What if the principal doesn't see the need for a father engagement program? This has happened to us many times. The first thing we did was try and find out *why* the administrator was resistant. Was it money, time, or something else?

The following are just a few of the reasons for resistance we've heard from school leaders:

- Administrators are swamped and can't add a single thing to their plates.
- The school doesn't have money for extra resources or programs.

- Many of the students come from single-mother homes and the presence of fathers would make them feel left out.
- Many dads are juggling multiple jobs just to support their families, and it would be an imposition to bother them.
- Most students are doing well academically and don't present any behavioral challenges, so why bother?
- Many of the students' fathers are incarcerated and would not be able to attend events.
- The fathers of students who most need them to be engaged refuse to do so—that's part of why these students need help in the first place.
- Mothers are the ones who care for children and are therefore the parents who should engage most with school.
- Staff hasn't received the necessary professional training.
- The school is very diverse and doesn't have enough educators who speak the fathers' languages or understand their cultures.

Regardless of their reasons for skepticism or hesitation, we went ahead and actively met with school administrators to discuss implementing a father engagement program. Each time, we started off by expressing our firm and abiding conviction that true change requires faith, determination, and resolve; a commitment to inclusion; a desire to push against old and discredited thinking; and a conviction that dads make a difference in the lives of their children and in the success of our schools. We made it clear that father engagement was not a luxury to seek only under ideal circumstances; it's a necessity to address students' academic or behavioral problems. Ironically, the excuses we heard most often for *not* starting a father engagement program—fathers are busy or poor, or they don't live at home—are among the reasons that the presence of committed male role models in schools is so important.

MATTHEW

"I will continue to make my presence known. That is something I missed when I was younger. Simple things, like being at Senior Night and not having a dad there to stand next to me, things like that. I just want my children to know that I am always going to be there for them as long as I am on this earth."

The presence of dads in school can have a salutary effect on teachers and staff, too, by making the school environment more inviting to all. Maybe you have noticed that teachers teach better when there are more eyes on them. This might be explained by "the company effect"—the way everyone tends to be on their best behavior when "company" is around. Well, something similar seems to go on when dads are in the building regularly! Students are more likely to follow school and district expectations. In fact, everyone—administrators, teachers and support staff—want to make a good impression on fathers and show their school in as positive a light as possible; even cafeteria workers will take extra care to present the food in an appealing way when there are visitors in the building. Courtesy and professionalism flourish when fathers are around. Everyone puts their best foot forward when they know dads are watching.

SAMUEL

"My daughters know that no matter what, I am there to support them. They can come to me about anything. Being open with my daughters allows them to see that Daddy is human. I can make mistakes. Allow that grace if you are trying: 'I may not hit that mark, but I am doing my best.'"

Finally, if your initial efforts are met with pushback, we also recommend reaching out to schools that have successfully implemented their own father engagement programs for guidance and data showing their programs' effectiveness. You can even ask to attend one of their fathers' meetings to get ideas and feedback from the fathers involved. Whatever you do, be persistent. The rewards are worth the effort.

In the next chapter, we'll get specific and look at a collection of strategies that your school can employ to set up and sustain effective and rewarding father engagement.

CHAPTER

Father Engagement Strategies

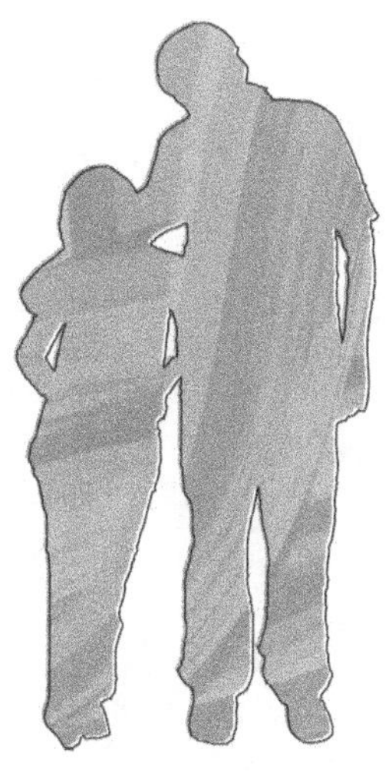

Many schools start the year strong when it comes to parent engagement, but activities and participation tend to wane after big events held early in the school year. Our recommendations for you are designed to sustain father engagement all year long and build their commitment to school partnership year after year. This is a deliberate choice. To ensure that, we used an application of a model developed by family engagement specialist Karen Mapp (in Mapp & Bergman, 2019) in conjunction with the Harvard Graduate School of Education.

There are two components of Mapp's model, called the Dual Capacity-Building Framework for School–Family Partnership, that we want to highlight for educators who might use it to guide their efforts: the recommended *process* conditions and the recommended *organizational* conditions for effective school–family collaboration:

- The *process* of family engagement should be culturally responsive, respectful, and relational, which means teachers and families see themselves as partners in the child's learning and development rather than as a service provider and a client. It is through close relationships that teachers can learn about and understand the strengths and conditions of their students' families.
- The *organization* of family engagement efforts should be systemic, embraced by leadership, integrated into the school's learning and improvement plans, and embedded in both professional development strategies and curriculum design. When planning new programs, policies, and activities, schools should be deliberate in their consideration of families (and, in our eyes, fathers especially) and should have plans in place to sustain family engagement with dedicated resources and infrastructure.

The results component of Mapp's approach is based on Monica Higgins's (2005) Four *C*s framework, which identifies four factors critical to sustaining an organization over the long term (Boudreau, 2020). Mapp explains that the benefits of engagement can be seen in increases in these factors, and we contend that schools best engage both families and school staff by addressing these components:

1. **Capabilities**—The specific skills and knowledge that families and educators must possess to work together successfully.
2. **Connections**—The webs and networks of trust on which partnership is built.
3. **Confidence**—Educators' and families' belief in their respective abilities and faith that their contributions will make a real difference.
4. **Cognition**—The shared understanding, values, and mental models that capture the way schools and families perceive each other and collaborate.

The strategies for father engagement we present in this chapter meet both Mapp's and Higgins's criteria. We've categorized them to help you create a balanced slate of father engagement activities that will sustain their partnership long term (see Figure 4.1). Although schools are free to pick and choose whichever strategies they'd like to use, if you are starting a father engagement program from scratch, we suggest you start with the ones that focus most on *capabilities* and *connections*. These are the easiest to implement and require comparatively less prep work.

To accommodate a variety of schedules, we recommend scheduling some activities during the day, some after school, and some (staff contracts permitting) on weekends. Remember that remote meeting technology, such as Zoom or Google Meet, can help to expand participation. We do recommend you avoid scheduling meetings during major sports events that are being televised or during times when local sports leagues practice or play. We learned that the hard way.

FIGURE 4.1
Father Engagement Strategies

Each of the engagement strategies below touches on all four aspects of Mary Higgins's Four *C*s framework but focuses most on the one under which it is listed.

 To Expand Capabilities	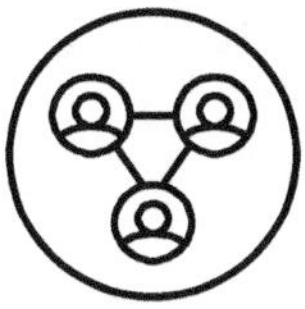 To Foster Connection	 To Build Confidence	 To Boost Cognition
• Message from Dad • Dads Teach Skills • Dads Do Math • Dads Read Books • Staff Appreciation Cookout	• Dads as Mentor • Dads PTA Meeting • Observational Walkarounds • Team Games • Dad Snack Attack • Dads Do SIP	• Dad Career Days • Dad Clap-Ins & Coffee Chats • Dad Chaperones • Dad Sports Program • Dads Attend Student-Led Conferences	• Dad Walks and Mini-Walks • Dads on District-Level Committees • Dads as End-of-the-Year Assistants • Phone Fathers First • Dad Posters

Many of these strategies are simple and will come naturally to both schools and fathers; others may require planning and training to ensure a truly collaborative relationship among fathers, students, and school. All are stepping stones that can be modified as needed to maintain a productive father engagement program. Pick and choose the ones that work best for your school, and try to connect them to any existing academic improvement plans.

To Expand Capabilities

The following engagement activities provide fathers with opportunities to contribute their skills, knowledge, and wisdom. In doing so, they help to expand your school's overall instructional capacity.

Message from Dad

This strategy provides fathers with an opportunity to serve as a positive male voice of encouragement, for both their own children and the other students at school.

Invite dads to record audio or video messages encouraging the students to do their best. After reviewing each submission, the school can broadcast these messages over the PA system or on school televisions or computer monitors. Throughout the school year, you might solicit more specific kinds of encouragement focused on specific topics (e.g., high-stakes tests, student relationships, school safety procedures) and develop a regular schedule for broadcasting them. You can even invite dads in to deliver their messages in person and videotape them as evidence of their commitment.

Dads Teach Skills

Fathers have all kinds of practical, real-world skills that might interest and empower students. These might be manual craft skills, such as woodworking, plumbing, carpentry, auto mechanics, or household maintenance. Other kinds of expertise they might pass on to students include how to code a website, data analysis, and how to write a technical article. Fathers can be a great source of artistic enrichment, helping students learn to play a musical instrument, create a video, learn to dance, paint a mural, or tell a story. These activities foster both appreciation for diversity as well as appreciation for craftsmanship.

We've seen schools present these instructional sessions on special occasions (see Dads Do Math and Dads Read Books). The skills typically vary by the ages of the students at school. Dads at an elementary school, for example, might focus on more basic or craft-oriented skills, with sessions on topics like how to repot plants, how to paint a birdhouse, or how to ride a bicycle. At the middle school level, they might teach students how to change a bike tire or how to write a social media post. Dads might teach high school students more career-related skills like how to write a business plan or how to patch a hole in a wall.

By facilitating these opportunities, schools are asserting that all fathers have knowledge and wisdom to impart. This strategy also allows fathers to provide both students and staff with visual affirmation of their investment. When they take time from their schedule to engage in this way, they signal the value they place on education.

Dads Do Math

This strategy is just what it sounds like—a math night that showcases fathers. It's a just-for-fun event or a friendly competition in which students and dads collaborate to solve interactive math problems. They might undertake problem-solving games, such as math escape rooms; measuring exercises; or math applications, such as budgeting, cooking, or building simple structures. They might work on timed puzzles, engage in solution relays, or embark on scavenger hunts in which every math problem solved is a clue. Dads Do Math makes a great addition to the usual preparations for mandated standardized testing.

There are endless ways to make this event feel special. We recommend taking photos of dads working with students to put up around the school or inviting a photographer to take portrait photos. Parent–child teams who "win" events or complete a certain number of tasks correctly might have their portrait posted in a "Math Solvers Hall of Fame" for the entire school year. You can also use this event to provide fathers with up-to-date information about the school's math curriculum and share strategies they can use to help their kids with schoolwork at home.

Teachers or coaches can wrap up the evening by praising everyone and making notes of how these exercises correlate with the kind of critical thinking that students use in class. This type of activity assists fathers to understand that mathematics is not just about problems and worksheets, but problem solving and exploring different strategies. It's also a way to boost students' math confidence while strengthening bonds between them and their dads. Consider providing the fathers with reminder cards or strategies they can use at home to prompt their children to reflect on how they approach challenges, to persevere through setbacks, and to value effort along with correct answers.

Note that you can adapt this approach to different subject areas: Dads Do Science, Dads Do Social Studies, and so on. A Dads Do Science night, for example, might feature hands-on experiments. A Dads Do Social Studies night might include map games or history trivia. The whole purpose is to make learning enjoyable, get everyone involved, and build genuine connections between dads and their children.

Dads Read Books

Designed for elementary and middle schools, a Dads Read Books event is a way for fathers to model literacy engagement in fun and meaningful ways. At the event, after greeting participating dads and students, teachers, a librarian, or a literacy coach shares the importance of family reading time and stresses that reading is more than a school task.

What about logistics? When this event is held at a school, groups can meet in several classrooms or a large space, such as a media center, cafeteria, or gym. The participating dads might choose their reading material from a collection of titles that are aligned with the curriculum or current reading themes, or they might be invited to bring in a book or story that is personally meaningful. The reading itself should be done in dad-led groups rather than in pairs of one dad and one student; this is a way to include students whose fathers cannot physically come in due to schedule conflicts, illness, travel, incarceration or death. And Dads Read Books can also be conducted virtually, with dads reading books to entire classes of students. We recommend recording these live reading sessions and making them available for replay.

You are probably familiar with the American Library Association's READ campaign, built around posters of famous people promoting reading. At Dads Read Books events, consider taking photos of dads holding a book—maybe reading with their child, reading to a group of children, or reading alone—and turning these photos into posters. They might feature the standard "READ" slogan (as if the dads were celebrities participating in the campaign) or variations like "Dads Who Read Lead" or "We Read Together!" Display these posters in school hallways or in the library to inspire students, celebrate fathers' engagement, and encourage other fathers to engage. Deborah did this at her school, and the dads' READ posters were a huge hit. Students and parents came to school to take photos beside the posters. The dads were instant celebrities.

Staff Appreciation Cookout

Invite fathers to set up grills and cook lunch for staff on professional development days. It's a great way for fathers to give back and show off their grilling skills and to have some low-stress conversations with school staff.

This is meant to be a fun event for all involved—a cooperative effort rather than an obligation for any participant. The school might provide simple supplies (e.g., hot dogs, burgers, or kebabs), and fathers can provide their time, culinary and organizational skills, and hospitality. Options for this event include contacting a local supermarket to solicit donations or asking the PTA to fund the food, drinks, and snacks.

To Foster Connection

The following engagement activities are especially effective at fostering a sustained school–home partnership.

Dads as Mentors

Students without any positive male role models in their lives benefit from being assigned a trusted male adult volunteer as a mentor. Schools should always get the consent and advice of the student's guardian before assigning male volunteers to students in this capacity. We recommend these relationships be set up as one mentor to multiple students rather than one mentor to one student. Each situation will be different and must be handled tactfully and with compassion.

Fathers considered for mentorship should all have demonstrated their dependability by showing up for past events, and they should have proven rapport with students. At your family and dad-focused events, look for the men to whom students tend to gravitate.

Once the mentorship is established, mentors can show up at students' performances or games to cheer them on, assist with classroom projects, and more. With a guardian's permission, students and mentors can meet regularly to discuss whatever is on the students' minds. For elementary school students, we recommend a staff member be present during these meetings.

Dads PTA Meeting

Invite fathers to a PTA (or PTO) meeting just for them, one focused on communicating specifically to dads about what is going on in the school and how they can help. Note that this session is not about "leaving out" mothers or current PTA members; it's an invitation and an introduction for fathers who are not members of the PTA and may not know how to become involved. In our experience, lots of dads never consider joining this group, believing the PTA is already set up or mostly run by moms—which is often true! In one sense, this is outreach intended to expand overall PTA participation. Getting dads involved is also strategic, as the PTA might have funds that pay for dad-focused events and activities, like the ones in this chapter. This event, which you might promote as a "A PTA Preview for Dads" or "Dads' Info Night," can be created as a relaxed atmosphere where fathers can learn about the PTA, ask their questions, and discover how they can make a significant difference.

Some schools schedule this event to take place on the same night as another school event—an hour before or right after a concert, a sports event, parents' night, or the like. The reasoning is that dads who are on campus anyway are more likely to stop in. In Deborah's experience, conducting the meetings for the fathers before events is better, because attendance will be higher. If a meeting is held after an event, parents are often tired and ready to get home to prepare for the following day.

Longer term, consider starting a PTA MORE committee; the MORE stands for Men Organized to Raise Engagement. This committee, a subgroup within your school's PTA, can focus on increasing father involvement in school activities and make sure dads are represented in the total school program, with at least one committee member attending all school meetings and events where parents are invited. This group could also sponsor fun father–child activities such as Dads Do Math, Dads Read Books, or mentorship programs. By bringing fathers into the PTA framework, your school is sending a powerful message: every parent's voice counts, and there's absolutely a place for dads at the table.

Observational Walkarounds

Schedule fathers to conduct observational walkarounds at the school. Allow them to have access to all classes, including their children's classes, and encourage them to walk the entire building the entire time they are there, both during and between classes. The only areas that should be off-limits are student bathrooms; make sure to let fathers know this and point them to staff bathrooms they can use.

This activity is a strategic way to build positive, collaborative relationships between staff and fathers. The presence of fathers also helps to keep the school safer and decreases internal truancy. Deborah has used this strategy at several schools and has had enormous success with it, especially in terms of decreasing negative student behaviors and helping to eliminate internal truancy.

Team Games

This strategy is about students and their fathers engaging in fun, competitive activities such as soccer, relay races, trivia contests, and STEM-building challenges. What it's really about is cooperative learning and enjoying the time together, which is a way for dads or children who would not normally be participating in organized team activities to do so.

The logistics are pretty simple. Teams are typically organized by teachers to be inclusive and fair—a mix of students, fathers, male role models, uncles, grandfathers, or any man who plays an active role in students' lives. Scheduling these events outside of 9-to-5 hours, on Friday evening or Saturday morning, is recommended.

Dad Snack Attack

This activity is a positive way for fathers to connect with school staff.

Schedule a time for fathers to visit the school and surprise staff with snacks, delivering them on a cart to each classroom and announcing, "Snack attack!" when they come in. You can contact the local supermarket to ask for donations or ask the PTA to provide the snacks.

Note that in this activity, no snacks are given to students. And although it might seem like that could lead to a lot of student grumbling, we've never seen it. What students generally do is stand and clap—after all, this is about appreciating teachers and school staff. Plus, students are "in on it" since their parents bring in the snacks. However, educators know their students best, and you might want to have small student gifts, like stickers or pencils on hand especially for elementary school students.

Dads Do SIP

Invite fathers to represent the community at meetings centered on school improvement planning (SIP) and share their insights into school culture and school–family partnership. Inviting fathers to serve in this role is validating; it shows them how much you value their voice.

It's also just good sense. Schools receiving federal funds are required to include family engagement strategies in their SIP, and this is an opportunity to collaborate with fathers on specific challenges schools are facing.

To Build Confidence

The following engagement activities are good ways to build fathers' belief in their respective abilities and assure them that their contributions are making a real difference.

Dad Career Days

Invite fathers for monthly lunches or small-group meetups where they can share how what they learned in school helped them in their careers. Out of consideration for fathers who may be embarrassed by their line of work, you can frame the activity as an invitation to talk about how what they learned in school relates to their specific jobs or how their job incorporates skills that students are building themselves, including critical thinking, problem solving, and collaboration.

If fathers cannot attend the school in person, encourage them to send in a two- to three-minute video of their response. You can also schedule virtual meetings for fathers to discuss their careers, answer any questions, and maybe even show students their work environment. The purpose of the event is twofold. Fathers have the opportunity to talk about their own personal careers and share what they learned in school and how that translates into work and life. Students learn about the variety of career opportunities available to them and about their dads' school and life experiences.

Dad Clap-Ins & Coffee Chats

Invite as many fathers as you can to come to school early to applaud students and staff as they enter the building and call out words of encouragement ("You got this!" "Have a great semester!" "Thanks for all you do!"). Then invite the men to stay for a "Dads Coffee Chat" with the school administration and teacher leaders. The presence of school staff demonstrates that the school values dad's input and gives dads a casual way to learn more about the school and how their engagement matters. This extra step transforms a moment of encouragement into a useful connection. Your aim in these chats is to help the fathers understand the school environment better and grasp that their presence and contributions make a difference.

This event can be scheduled quarterly and is especially well received on the first and last days of school. Afterward, be sure to recognize the fathers in your communications to families and the community.

Dad Chaperones

Invite fathers to chaperone field trips, where they have a chance to learn alongside their children while also assisting the teachers with supervision and logistics. Consider asking dad volunteers to "buddy up" with another father to make the experience more enjoyable and encourage teamwork. Working in pairs tends to give both dads more confidence, and this is especially appreciated by the dads who are first-time chaperones or first-time school volunteers. It also helps build the kind of overall "dad solidarity" that helps strengthen and sustain father engagement.

Although you may be tempted to have dad chaperones focus on supervising students with a history of misbehavior, we advise against this. Field trips are meant to be collective learning experiences, and you want students, teachers, and other parents to view the fathers not as disciplinarians but as facilitative learning partners. In their chaperone capacity, they are reaffirming their presence as positive and encouraging rather than as rule enforcers.

Dad Sports Program

Whereas the Team Games strategy is a friendly competition, this program is purely for fun. Invite dads to visit

Afterword

JOSEPH

"Having my dad at home growing up, I always counted it like a blessing. The idea of me becoming a father was like, *Ohh man.* I was nervous. My dad did the best that he could, and he taught me a lot, but now I'm in his place. I'm responsible. I know I won't fail my kids, but the thought that I could does come up. I want to be present for them. I want to build them to be mentally strong so they can be vulnerable and so they can communicate with me whenever they're feeling something—whatever it is, whether they are sad or happy, mad or angry. And not just my daughter but my sons, as well. Society does not see men as really having emotions; being a man is always about being tough, right? And in some instances, being tough is important, but it's important also to be able to do what we're doing right now, which is communicate about how we feel, how we've felt, at different times in our lives. I don't have the trauma of growing up without dad, but I do have the pressures of being a good father. I think about that. When my kids get older, I want them to look back and say, 'Not just my mom but my dad, too, definitely loved me, and he celebrated me, and in love he also corrected me. He lets me know when some things are not right and how we can fix it.'"

We wrote this book to help schools engage fathers in their children's education because we know, both from the research and from our own experiences, that father engagement is essential to children's academic, social, and emotional well-being.

Being a parent can push one to their limits. As Chacko can attest, men tend to keep their thoughts and feelings private. Social conditioning can make it feel awkward to express the deep care they feel for their families. From a male perspective, talking openly about these experiences can be tough; many men carry unspoken joys and struggles because they're unsure how to share them. That's why spaces where men can speak honestly with one another are so important. When fathers gather and realize they're not alone in their questions, fears, and hopes, a sense of solidarity forms. In that shared understanding, men find encouragement, strength, and the courage to grow into the fathers their children need.

Too many dads who want to encourage, reassure, apologize to, and celebrate their children do not do so. And the children notice their fathers' actions, presence, and absence, more than many fathers realize. The exact activities that fathers engage in with their children matter less than the fact of their availability and proximity, both physically and emotionally. For a child, just sitting together with Dad, listening to a story, or sharing silence can communicate safety and love in powerful ways. A father's presence is a steady anchor in the world.

While schools did not create the trauma of fatherlessness, schools have a chance to be a place of healing for students (and dads) who are in this cycle of pain. Students may not be able to articulate their need for more male teachers, male staff members, and for their father's presence in school, but it's up to educators to spearhead the change. This is a time to purposefully hire more male educators at all grade levels, preK–12. This is the time to intentionally engage with fathers and to invite them to regularly be a part of school decisions. It is time for schools to do a self-check and build awareness. Schools must take a moment to reflect on their practices, question their viewpoints, and decide whether their present actions create room for fathers to be acknowledged as partners in their children's success. It's time to explore ways to make sure not just mothers but fathers are engaged in their child's school.

Fathers, whose voices are heard and who are genuinely engaged in decision making, are not only recognized but also feel that their presence is acknowledged when schools incorporate them in an active way. Such schools convey a powerful signal that dads are not on the periphery but are indeed considered as co-parents in the educational and developmental progress of their children.

When schools facilitate the presence and input of fathers, they send fathers the message that they share responsibility for their children's success. By working together, administrators, educators, dads, and other family members can ensure children get the balanced support they need to thrive. We hope the context, guidance, and strategies in this book will help you and your school meet this goal.

If schools do not engage fathers, it is a great loss.
If schools *do* engage fathers, the results are invaluable.

Acknowledgments

From Chacko

This book is written with deep gratitude to God, who has guided every step of my journey as a father. In moments of uncertainty and in moments of joy, His grace has been the foundation that shaped my understanding of love, responsibility, and purpose. This work exists because of His faithfulness.

I am especially grateful to my wife, Indu, whose strength, wisdom, and unwavering support have been my constant encouragement. You have been my partner in every sense of the word, and your love has shaped both our family and the heart behind these pages.

To our children, Elias, Maya, and Zara . . . you are the reason this book was written. You have taught me more about patience, joy, humility, and love than any words ever could. Being your father is the greatest privilege of my life, and this book is a reflection of the lessons you continue to teach me every day.

I am also deeply thankful for Deborah, whose encouragement and support helped sustain this journey. Your belief in this work and the vision behind it has meant more than words can express.

Finally, I am grateful to the many fathers who generously shared their stories, struggles, and victories. Your honesty and courage shaped these pages, and this book exists because of your willingness to open your hearts and walk this journey together.

From Deborah

I thank God for his hand all over this book in turning the hearts of fathers back to their children.

I thank God for Chacko. I would not have co-written a book without his prodding.

I dedicate this book to my late parents, Wheeler Winstead, Sr., and Barbara Winstead Mills, who passed a few months before publication.

I am grateful for the support from my husband, Thomas Higdon, Jr., who also says, "You got this!" I am grateful for my son, Harold Hall, III; my daughter-in-love, Morgan; and my granddaughters, Loriana and Aria. I love you always and in all ways!

I am thankful for my wonderful siblings for their unwavering support and to all the family and friends who encouraged me throughout this process.

I am also grateful for the following fathers we interviewed whose voices will help spur more schools to engage dads: Karis Chandler; Harold Hall, III; Michael-Anthony James; Calvin Jenkins, Jr.; Warren Palmer, II; Kolten Perine; Maurice Polk; D'Juan Terry; and Larry Tolson.

To God be the Glory!

APPENDIX

Father Interviews

We conducted a total of three interviews (two via videoconference and one in person), talking with the subjects in groups of three or four. All interviews took place between December 4 and December 12, 2021. Each man sat for a single interview with the exception of Samuel, who was interviewed twice. We have changed the subjects' names to protect their privacy.

The Subjects

- Thomas, 36, is married with one son (7) and one daughter (4). He grew up without a father at home.
- Samuel, 37, is married with two daughters (7). He grew up without a father at home.
- John, 37, is married with two sons (5 and 3). He grew up with both parents at home.
- David, 38, is married with one daughter (5) and a son on the way. He grew up without a father at home.
- Joseph is 35, married with two sons (7 and 15 months) and one daughter (3). He grew up with both parents at home.
- Matthew, 37, is married with three daughters (15, 13, and 5) and one son (6). He grew up without a father at home.
- Benjamin, 29, is married with one daughter (3) and another child on the way. He lived with both parents until they divorced when he was 8.
- Lucas, 31, is unmarried with one son (8) and one daughter (6) by two women. He grew up without a father at home.
- Peter, 35, is divorced with two daughters (8 and 6). He grew up without a father at home.

Question 1: What was the impact, or lack of impact, that your father had on your education?

Thomas: Good question. My dad raised eight kids. [*Authors' note:* As a child, Thomas did not live with his father.] His impact was tremendous. He knew that a poor education was going to separate us from the things that we wanted out of life. So, his impact was tremendous. He was the type of guy who, if you brought home a *C,* that was failing. He stayed on us. If I needed help with a subject, he would reach out to all resources and try to get me help, tutoring, and all that type of guidance. But if we didn't say nothing and then brought home a *C, that* was an issue. He stayed on us. My mom wasn't a stickler like my dad was. She was more nurturing and caring about it. She sat down and tried to help me. But my dad was the stickler. It rubbed off on me and still has an impact on my children now.

Samuel: My story is kind of the opposite. I didn't have a father—my own father—to check up on me with grades. I think that that played a role in how I did in school. Granted, I had a tremendous mom who was amazing. She made sure I had my grades right. She put the load on that! But there were many times when I wished I could have had a dad to check up on my grades and make sure. Like, "Hey! How are your grades doing?" and kind of put that hand down. But when I was a child, and even now as an adult, I did have great father figures in my uncles and some of my friends' dads. They really stepped up for me. Now that I am a father, I use the tools that I learned from my uncles and from some of my friends' dads to guide me.

David: Same thing with me. I was raised in a single-parent household, and I never got to meet my dad. The environment I was in with my mom was an environment where there were high expectations regardless. That was something that pushed me ahead, as far as a trajectory. I did, however, have an uncle who I spent summers with for 8 or 10 years. Just by God's grace, he introduced me to technology when I was about 8 years old. In my regular vicinity in Brooklyn, I had zero access to technology. It was something to walk by and marvel at but not have access to. But when I went to my uncle's place in Jersey, I had a plethora of technology at my disposal. I am talking mid-'80s. I learned how to use floppy discs and everything from there. So, I had a jump-start on life. I was just lucky. It was a matter of things falling in place.

John: My dad worked most of the day. He would leave early and drop me off at school around 6:30 or 7:00 a.m. and would not come home until the evening around 7:00. He worked an hour away, so my mom took the lead on my education. But at the same time, my dad would always, kind of before dropping us off every day, say, "Hey, let me know if you need help in any subject" or what not. When he would get home, he would kind of check in, make sure our homework and projects were done, see if we needed help studying in any specific subjects or anything like that. Even though he wasn't the lead parent in education—if there was a parent–teacher conference, it was usually my mom in there—it was good to know that they were on the same page and continually being there and showing support. As my two sons grow up and they get into the more academic stuff, I want to be there for them. Then it carries over to the guys I coach and mentor now, too.

Samuel: I grew up in a single-parent household, so my father was not there, and a lot of the load fell on my mother. As a child, I didn't look at [his absence] a lot, but I *felt* it, if that makes any sense. I would see other friends—and, as I got older, classmates—who had their fathers, and I would feel it personally a little more. My father did not have a role in my life at all. So that affects my parenthood even today.

Joseph: The impact of my father on my education was that he was a high school graduate who did not follow the path from high school to college. He did some college later, as I got older. He always voiced the idea of me taking my education seriously. He shared that even though he had potential, he didn't always do his best, and that changed his path. It made his life harder. As a result, he instilled the importance in me of always doing my best, giving my best, and taking advantage of opportunities while they are available.

Benjamin: I grew up knowing my dad. I lived with him and my mom until they divorced when I was 8. Then he moved out of state, but I still saw him occasionally. I went to live with him when I was in high school, but it was rough, and I ended up moving out and living with relatives. For my personal education, I could have succeeded more if my dad had been involved, but I had to be self-sufficient. With me being self-sufficient in my own education, I did things my own way. I am not saying that my dad didn't care, but he didn't invest his time enough for me to be as good as I should've been in school. I had to have my own self-discipline and stuff like that, and I kind of fell off. My dad got upset when I fell off.

Lucas: My dad didn't really come around until after my high school years, so it was mostly phone calls with him where he said things like, "If the grades are not good, you are not going to get a toy or a gift." My dad was not really there—only with phone calls—so he didn't impact my education.

Peter: I didn't really have a chance with my father. He didn't really make an impact. I had to learn how to do everything on my own. My mother was single, and I had to help with bills. So, to be honest, I had to drop out of school. I really had to drop out of school and get a GED. I didn't get my GED until years later. I had to discipline myself. That was the impact. My father not being there gave me the push to know that I can be a better man. He just wasn't there, and that played a big part in my elevation.

Question 2: What will you specifically do that your father or father figure did that had an impact on you?

Samuel: The accountability. There were times when my uncles would pull me aside and be like, "Hey, what's *x*, *y*, and *z*?" and be firm about it. I knew that I had a certain period of time to get *x*, *y*, and *z* right. I looked forward to them doing that, because it meant they were watching me in certain ways and that they remembered how I was doing. That is one aspect—accountability. Then also just being real. Them telling me about how they navigated through a few things. Understanding that if I didn't hit the mark, that it was OK—*this too shall pass*. But also letting me know that I had to hit that mark, too. It was like, "Even if you don't hit it now, do your best to get back." The accountability aspect and the empathy. A good ear to let you know that you can make it. But also the perseverance. Like, "Hey, it's time to pick up the pieces and to keep going."

John: Yes, I think the impact on me was one of the things that Samuel touched on, the accountability. Being accountable for your failing and for your success. It was my dad teaching me that throughout school—*you get out what you put in.* Then, also, I think about him allowing me to fail. Allowing me to learn from the failures and not hand-holding me through things. Giving me the tools first, asking me if I need any help or support, and letting me go. Then I come back to how he stressed not getting frustrated, not getting overly joyful, but learning from struggle so I could be more successful the next time. One last thing he taught me by example was to always be accessible. No matter what he was doing, he was accessible to me. He would always take a few minutes to walk me through something or show me how something is done, that type of deal. So, I think those are the three things that I definitely want to carry on with my kids—both my biological kids and the kids I work with, coach, and train.

Thomas: I'll touch on two things my dad did that I will probably do with my kids. My dad was super-hands-on. Just seeing his presence, him walking through my school, let me know to act right. Him being on a first-name basis with the teachers, them knowing that he was checking in. He didn't wait for the progress reports; he was hands-on. He was there at parent–teacher conferences. He even started working at my school. I don't know if I would go to that extent, but I will definitely be present with my kids. Next important lesson was not being scared to reach out for resources. If I needed study sessions, or if I needed mentoring, he would reach out and try to find those resources. I am definitely going to instill that in my son—not to be scared to ask for help. *Dad can go find help if you need some help. I can go find it for you, for sure.*

David: Nothing, because my dad and I didn't have that kind of interaction. One of the things that I would continue to push is fluidity. Education happens at school, and it also happens at home. So, I will be preparing my son and daughter for a multitude of situations as opposed to putting so much stock in the school environment alone. While it is important, and they will have to do well there in school, they will have to also be prepared for the world ahead. As older men now, I think we are starting to be aware that the system leaves some gaps, and we have to fill some of those gaps.

Samuel: I would piggyback on what David said. I wouldn't do anything my father did, since my father wasn't around.

Breaking that curse and breaking that tradition is something that I've made a point to do for my daughters.

Joseph: Actually, a couple things come to mind. One thing is continuing to value hard work, and the other comes from thinking about when I was younger, and there was a point when we were in school, and we were talking about "the new math." My parents didn't fully understand it, so they wanted to help me but could only help me to a certain point. When they didn't feel that *they* could help me any longer, they sought out help. Whether it was tutors or some of the older high school students, when I was in middle school, my parents got me someone who was able to help. They would talk to them and ask them to tutor me in math when I was struggling or tutor me in English when I was struggling. Those are the two things that I would actually continue to do: teach my children to value hard work and to advocate for themselves. And I advocate for them if they need additional support.

Lucas: I am going to do better than my dad did by staying in my own kids' lives every day, calling and talking to them. By helping them with homework. But I am not physically there every day for my two children. They live with their moms. So, I call on a regular basis, because I have to stay on top of it every day.

Peter: I am there every step of the way. I call my kids every day. I call them whenever. I am overprotective. I am there morally. People may feel that to be a father, you only have to be there and give materialistic things, but it takes more morally. So that's what I am doing: morally, I am there for them to make them mentally strong. I feel that my generation didn't have that. No one was there to be strong for us.

Benjamin: As a kid, I wasn't as vocal, but as a father, I am not going to hover over my daughter but watch over her and see where she may need guidance.

Question 3: What is something your father did—or didn't do—that you will change?

John: That's a tough one. I think I want to do what Thomas said before— be more hands-on. Be more visible. Not to say that I would not step back and let my boys do their thing, but I want to be more visible with the teachers and at the schools so that they know that if I can be there, I'll be there.

Samuel: Because my father was not present, just being present is something that I definitely will change. I will be an ear. Let my daughters know that I am approachable, let them know that it's OK that something may happen, that I am here for them and supporting them, no matter what, and I just want to love up on them. I think that's one of the hardest things for fathers to get. Sometimes we want to be so tough. I want them to know that I love them regardless of anything. And so just being there and loving them and just showing that support are things that I will definitely do.

Thomas: This is a good question. I don't think I will probably change much. I think my father laid out a blueprint that I will probably follow, just knowing that it worked. Having eight kids, and all eight went to college . . . I think the blueprint worked. I think I may be a little bit more affectionate; my dad was a stickler. But I don't want my son to walk over me, either. I will sit down and hear him out, because sometimes growing up, I was told, "You will do this," and I did it. Other than that, I think the blueprint was great. I wouldn't change much.

Joseph: I will, one, continue to push myself to be the best that I can be. And I say that in terms of not shying away from opportunities that are meant for me, even if they may seem overwhelming or very taxing. I want my children to see the value of hard work. I also want to show them that there is really no real failure if you have tried your best. Also, the ideas of persistence and resilience. Showing them that something might be complicated at first, but there are ways to work through it. I want them to know that they don't have to struggle alone . . . that I can need support and solicit support, and they can do the same thing for themselves and be supported by me.

Samuel: Kind of the same thing everyone is saying . . . just being there. *Being present is better than presents.* I say that all the time. My daughters know that no matter what, I am there to support her. She can come to me about anything. Being open with my daughters and having that open communication is so important. Also allowing them to see that Daddy is human. I can make mistakes and that's OK—like you said, Joseph. If you are trying, allow yourself grace. *I may have not have hit that mark, but I am doing my best.* One thing that I am intentional about doing is telling my oldest daughter that I am sorry. A lot of times, as fathers, we don't admit that we made a mistake. When I don't hit the mark, I apologize. I ask her, "Do you forgive me?" I give my daughters that grace as well. Also, I let them see that I love their mother.

David: Samuel shares some of the same philosophy as I do. The environment is key. I'm about making sure that they see tons of positive imagery about me and their mom, because that's where they gain their identity. I remember a lot of times, I was looking for myself in my environment and I couldn't find it. We did not travel much. My mom didn't date often. So, I was looking for that. I think another one for me is that I will continue to live a fulfilling life. And there's a two-prong approach to that. Number one, I show them how to get after it, how to go for their dreams. You only have one life to live. And we all know that many people live as if they have another one on the way. A reason I do that is that I don't put my unfulfilled dreams on my kids. They have to be allowed to seek whatever their heart's desire is, and it is not on me to hit the "continue button" through them. If there is something that I can influence and they want to take to the next level, then by all means, that's a beautiful thing. But I don't believe in passing the baton unless it's wanted.

Question 4: How are you currently involved in your child's education?

Thomas: In this day and age, the communication between the teachers and the parents is a little bit easier than having to walk up into the school. I have an app. I talk to my son's teachers all the time. I am present. I let her know that if there are any issues, she can reach out to me. I work close to the school, and I will even come up there if need be. I am present in every aspect. If there is a parent–teacher conference, my wife makes sure I am there as well. If it is after-school activities, I am there. If it is school projects, I am there. I can say I am highly involved. My dad did it for me, and I am going to continue that blueprint. The school extended the opportunity to read out loud to the kids and things like that, and I am super-involved. I've never shied away from being present and being there.

Samuel: Kind of like what Thomas was saying, I definitely make sure that when my daughter gets home, we have a quick little talk, just checking in. *How was your day? What are some things you learned?* That way, she knows that I am tuned in to what she is doing daily. She also knows that I want her to be paying attention in school because retention is key. I have a new daughter, and even now . . . what Thomas was saying about reading to his daughter? I am reading to mine, and she is only three weeks old. I am constantly doing little things with my older daughter, like flash cards, multiplication and division, those little things. I think me being a teacher plays into it. I have the benefit of being on the other side. These are the things I do with my daughters. I am on the emails, and I'm in constant communication with her teacher. It's letting her know that she is supported, that she has a father who is there. And it's even letting the other kids at school know that she has a father who is there, so there isn't any problem with them.

John: Yes, to echo what Samuel and Thomas said, something I'm doing is being involved with the preK. I usually drop off my son in the mornings to his preK. I am able to talk to his teacher for a second, and they know that if they need me, they just need to let me know, and I will be there. We are connected to the school through an app, too, so communication is pretty quick. I've been to all of my son's parent–teacher conferences, and I'm keeping up with his development and education. He wants to learn, so he brings home this big book of education stuff to help his development, and we go through it together. I also think that providing is an example for him. So is how I love up on his mom, how I talk to her, how we interact in the community and at home. Then there's discipline—that's a big thing as well. It's like, say please and thank you. When you want to talk to an adult and they are talking to somebody else, you say, "Excuse me" and wait. Some of the niceties in life that I grew up with, I want to pass that on. My family enforced them, and my dad enforced them. When my son is out in public, I know people are like, "That is a well-behaved, respectful young man." It's kind of weird that I am the strict parent. I never thought that would happen.

Question 5: There is a major crisis with behaviors in schools, especially with boys. They use inappropriate language; they are often physically aggressive, even destructive. Schools are also seeing more students acting out sexually. Schools are seeing students coming to school in a rage—and not just secondary schools; recently, it has been elementary students as young as those in kindergarten to 2nd grade. What is going on? We are seeing this especially with students who either have no father in the house or a non-involved mother's boyfriend in the house. What can we do?

Thomas: Mentorship is needed. They need positive role models and sports. Little kids are a product of their environment; if you can get them out of those tough situations and around some positive people, maybe that can change them. It's hard to say, because the parents have to be onboard with it as well. And the kids have to be on board. Can't force them to do it. I think the key is to get them around positive models with positive reinforcements.

John: You touched on it. The message at home has to be consistent with the message at school and the message from mentors. When I was working at a middle school, I loved looking over at male staff members and some of the other young men working with these students in resource class. The kids would listen to us. They looked up to us. Sometimes the conversations we had weren't easy or great. Sometimes they didn't react positively to what we had to say. I think having mentors in the school environment to kind of guide and have those "tough love conversations" with them is a must. The lack of that is why I think we have some of these issues in schools. I agree with Thomas about mentorship and making that a focus in some of our hiring in schools. It is absolutely a priority. It's key.

Samuel: Yes, just to piggyback on what Thomas and John were saying, being actually in the schools, I see this: students, especially males, who are hurting. I can relate, because I was a young man who was hurting. You find ways to make it. In this day and age, there's not the outlet for these kids that there was before. And the problem seems to be more prevalent. We have to change the narrative. At one point, it was a cool thing to go without. It was a cool thing to have someone say, "Man, you don't have this." But then it became, over time, a stigma. That's a trauma I see. I have tried to change that mentality—that *it's cool; I don't need a father* mentality—because I was like that. You know, *I don't need him.* It is trauma that is being masked. So, mentorship, constant mentorship, the tough conversations—you have to have that. The unconditional love? You have to have it. That's one thing that especially men are lacking, the love, because they don't see it. Whether the father isn't being affectionate enough, or the father is not there, and kids see love going to other people or in other directions, it makes you feel like, *Why me? What did I do?* Even at an early age, we all want some type of love and affection. When you see those young boys at the elementary school, a lot of the times these are students who are seeing things from a man in their life that are not positive. They are thinking this negative thing is love, or they are not seeing love at all. So, over time, those tough love conversations are something they need very much. I have also tried to be intentional in saying, "Hey, young man, I love you." I tell them, "I love you." Sometimes it kind of takes them off, because they may never have heard that from another male before. Now it has become a natural thing. They know I am coming from a great place. Thomas and John are both coaches, so I know the effect that their presence has when they walk in a room. They probably see that kids gravitate to them, because I see it, too. We are needed not just in the classroom but as coaches, in business mentorships, in business offices, in correctional facilities, in restoration facilities. We are needed everywhere!

Joseph: What can we do to help? We can be a role model for these students, celebrate their successes with them, correct them when they need correction, and be intentional about their mindset. We can build up how they view themselves—how they feel about themselves and how they feel about different tasks. We can make sure they know some things may be difficult and may require more work, but hard work's not something to shy away from or try to take the easy route around. We can build up their mindset to the point when they say, "I can do this."

Authors' Note: We continued with a follow-up conversation about trauma.

Dr. Higdon: Samuel, talk more about how you see a child not having a father in their life as trauma. . . .

Samuel: Not having a father is a constant. It can be a constant in a negative way, if you allow it to be. I know all four guys on this Zoom, collectively and individually, and we've talked about how we want to reprogram that. We want to reprogram what a father is. Me personally, I feel the trauma in a lot in little things: when I am taking my daughter to get her shots or making her food, or she's throwing up and I am making sure that she's OK, or I am doing laundry. Like, these little things sometimes can be a trigger. It can kind of mess with me a little bit. I've talked to David about that. I'll be honest, in the early stages of my fatherhood, little things like this, things I didn't have, were overwhelming. But I realized that I wanted to break that cycle. Sometimes it's still a sensitive topic with me. But it gets better when you have these types of conversations and you are vulnerable. It takes time. It's not something that you can rush, and you have to come to a comfortable place where you realize that it is what it is. You determine how to move forward so that your children don't feel those traumas that you experienced. What my father did was out of my control. I can allow that to control what I am doing now or not, and I choose not. That has been my saving grace more than anything. I'm cool.

Matthew: I am agreeing that it is a trauma, and it can mess up your mental. As a kid, sometimes I just felt, like, why didn't my dad want to be there? Was it me? That and other things you go through, you just wonder why. Why couldn't I have that? Me, I just turned it around, and I give my kids what I didn't have. I make sure my kids have that. I've talked to them about that, because they've asked. You know, "Dad, where is your dad?" It gets brought up a lot, especially by my 15- and 13-year-old daughters, so I can't just push it away like I can with the little kids. I have to have more of an intensive conversation with them. When it gets brought up, it definitely makes me sit and think. A lot of times, think, *At least I'm not* *becoming like my dad, and I'm doing everything to be the opposite of that.* I am being the best father I can for my kids. I am not perfect, but I am doing my best.

David: This idea of the absence of your father being a trauma is what I just sat with for the last five minutes. It certainly is. In fact, the impending birth of my son is bringing up new feelings about fatherhood that I thought I was cool on, right? I thought I had this handled. Now I got a son on the way, and it's like, *woooo.* The first thing that I have been hovering on is that I wish I had been anticipated the way I am anticipating him. When you talk about the trauma and all of that stuff, it's literally the *wanting.* Matthew, you made a point about your kids wanting to know who your dad is and some of the backstory. I have a journal that I am currently writing that I am going to present to my daughter when she turns 18. *The first thing is that I want you to know you were made in love.* I don't know what the story of my conception was. To know that you were created with intention, in a loving environment matters. There's a difference between *you are here for working servitude* versus *we are all here to experience this time together.* I think it really affects outcomes down the line.

Peter: It's definitely a trauma not having a father in your life to help guide you. It's like you are guessing every step of the way. You are really just guessing how to be a man. You have your mom and a couple of women you grew up with, but I feel like a man can teach me how to be a man. A male figure is needed in the discipline. A woman can do it, but a male figure makes that discipline really hit home. Without it I feel like, *wooo.* . . . If my father had been there, I probably would have finished school.

Benjamin: My dad was a disciplinarian—very much so, a very strict disciplinarian. Which made it hard for us to have a relationship, a true relationship. Now that I am older, we do have a good relationship. When I was younger, he was a disciplinarian, so the relationship factor wasn't there, because I had a fear about going to my dad. I had a fear of saying certain things to my dad as opposed to now, we can talk about things. We can even talk about those old things and have a good dialogue, whereas before, I was scared to do that. So, it is a trauma, and it stays with you a long time, but also I feel that it helps you with your kids because you know what not to do and what you should do, which is to have a relationship with your kids.

Lucas: It is traumatizing, but if you have your own desires—especially if your dad has a desire to connect with you, and you connect with one another—it makes it much easier. It is traumatizing in the beginning. I had a mom who was like a dad. For 16 years, she told me and my sister that we didn't have to worry about anything. "I got you. Until your dad comes around, you won't understand what is going on." She didn't bash my dad for not being there. She didn't bash him because, she said, "You will figure it out when you get older." Then my dad started talking to me, and now we have a great bond. He sat down and told me his explanation, and I told him how I felt. We have been close together ever since.

Joseph: It's interesting to me, hearing all of your stories. What my dad did for me is what you are doing for your kids. But even for me, having him there? I always counted it like a blessing. The idea of me becoming a father was like *oh man.* I was nervous because, again, my dad did the best that he could, and he taught me a lot, but now I'm in this place. I'm responsible—well, not just me, my wife and I are. I am responsible for a life times three. In the back of my mind, I know I won't fail them, but that thought comes up. I don't want to fail them. By being present and by not failing them, I am building them to be mentally strong. To be able to be vulnerable and be able to communicate with me whenever they're feeling something—and not just my daughter but my sons as well. Society does not see males as really having emotions; it's always about being tough. In some instances, toughness is important, but it's important to also be able to do what we're doing right now, which is communicate about how we feel. I want to instill in my kids the ability to talk through whatever it is they're feeling, whether they are sad or happy or mad or angry. I don't have the trauma, but I have the pressure of wanting to be a good father. I think about that. When it's all said and done, that's always my thought and my prayer. When my kids get older, I want them to look back and say, "Not just my mom but also my dad definitely loved me, and he celebrated me, and in love he also corrected me."

David: Those nerves [about being a good father] are a great thing. They let you know that your heart and your mind are very present, so don't even worry about it.

Joseph: That means you care, bro. That means you are on the right track.

Dr. Higdon: You say correction is key. I see that with some of the kids who are acting up. Some of these kids are trying to force our hand to force their family members to demonstrate that they care about them. My son felt more secure sleeping at my sister's house because my brother-in-law was there. My son did not sleep the same at our house because he felt he had to be alert in case someone came in the house and he had to defend us. It never crossed my mind that he might feel that way. I think that it is a powerful thing you just said about saying "I love you." Wow! I grew up hearing that a lot from my parents and my grandparents. As my father was getting older, he was aware that he was transitioning out of life. He would never end a conversation with his children without saying, "Remember I love you. Remember I love you." I wonder how many kids have never heard that from their parents, mother or father.

Thomas: It's crazy you say that, because even though my parents were both hands-on, they didn't say "I love you" a lot.

They didn't. But I always felt it, even if it was through gifts or them going the extra mile. It wasn't until I met my wife and saw how she interacted with her parents, saw that she said "I love you" after every conversation that this struck me. It's instilled in me now. I think sometimes it shocks my parents when I get off the phone by saying "I love you." The first time I said that, my mom was like, "Uh-huh, I love you, too." But it's natural now. It wasn't until I met my wife that I saw that those words are powerful, you know? I say it now before my daughter and son go to sleep. It seems like they sleep better. It's the knowing. It's weird when I *don't* say it.

Samuel: I am very active in my daughters' lives. When my first daughter was born . . . I am a teacher, so immediately I was reading to her. I am a math teacher, so now we're going over multiplication, we are doing angles, we are doing all types of things. But also . . . just checking in with her daily and asking what she learned, what are some things she likes, what her favorite subject is. . . . I believe all this lets her know that her father is in tune with what she is doing. I let her know so that she just doesn't go through her day without having any accountability. I know some kids who just go through the motions throughout the day, and there's no one checking on whether they are doing well or not doing well. I want to know if my daughter is having a great day or if she's not. Also, just going over her work, too. I communicate with her teachers. My wife and I, we do a good job of checking in with her teacher, so they also know it's both parents who are active. They know that she has a support system; that is also key. David and Joseph also piggybacked on this, but letting people know it's both of us matters. Sometimes, as fathers, we get that stigma that *oh, it's only the mothers that are doing it,* but now I see a lot of fathers involved. I see a lot of fathers in PTSA meetings, picking up children, and going to different school events. It's like we're breaking and changing that narrative.

David: I am involved in a multitude of ways. It all starts with having a great relationship with her teacher, really understanding that it's a partnership. I am very present in a way that I wish my dad had been. The "check-in" when I was growing up was to make sure you weren't embarrassing them. The tone was more about making sure I was on the path to get what was needed, leading from a path of correction. It really didn't feel good. I am glad that we are speaking about the positives. I am always encouraging my daughter. Every day I encourage her to try her best. *Don't give up!* If she needs a break, she should take it and give her best when she has more energy. The next thing is I am really big on the supplementary in education. Where Samuel is a math teacher, I am creative by day. So, we are constantly involved in tactiles. It is the art projects; it is DJing. She has a keyboard in here. We are constantly on some sort of hands-on way to get her emoting. Those are the little things we work on. Then also we bring it back to more rigorous parts—the flash cards and the quantitative part of education as well. One thing that I have started to do is a game we call "Daddy Quiz." If there is anything that I want her to remember, I give it to her in some sort of a game show/quiz format. If she is learning colors, for example, I would say, "What color is Grandpa's car? Is it (a) red, (b) silver, or (c) blue?" Through that repetition, over time I have been able to log in a lot of different concepts. I bring a playfulness to education, so that it makes it fun. I remember being drilled. It was an embarrassing situation. *We are on this journey together.* I want her to know that. *It's not that it is* your *job to learn; it is our job to learn together.* It's really about staying committed and walking hand-in-hand with her.

Joseph: What can I add? I agree with these gentlemen. Really, it's about being active and, to add to what was already said, being *present,* asking questions, checking in, and seeing what my kids can speak to in terms of what they learned in school today. My daughter is just 3, but I am trying to get her to tell me the activities that she is doing in her daycare. I am developing a conversation with my kids. Being able to talk about their day and not just hear "It was good." Being able to dig a little deeper. I love math, but I am also teaching science this year. My wife is not a teacher, but she is the hardcore reader and the writer in the family, so we are using both of our skill sets to help them. My son, he likes to read, but writing is a growth area for him, so my wife is having him write letters to his grandparents. He loves music, so he and I go back and forth with rapping and writing raps. I don't know where it came from, but he can write in freestyle from the top of his head. I have to write mine down and come back to him. We make it fun. He talks very well, but especially during the pandemic, the skill of writing was not as strong as it would have been. With the math . . . when I'm cooking, we just pull different math scenarios to make it relevant. Just before this meeting, I was sitting in with him because his school had a family coding night. They were doing an activity through a program called Scratch, talking about sequencing and algorithms. So I was learning like he was learning. It was an opportunity for us to share that and to learn and work together. Moments like that . . . I am hoping that as he gets older, he will remember them. Who knows what that might turn into for him?

David: Not to cut you off, but also there's one thing I remember that I have done with intention. I stopped reading books on my phone and went back to reading actual physical books so my daughter could see me reading a hard book.

Dr. Higdon: That modeling is such a powerful thing. Years ago, as an assistant principal, I started hosting father-and-son basketball games. Between games, the fathers shared a book that was significant to them. At one game, a Latino boy said he never knew Black men could read. He had never seen grown men, especially Black men, with a book in their hands, reading. He never saw them reading on social media, on TV, in movies, in advertisements. It still is true. Where do we see men reading or reading to their children? At my school, fathers did READ posters with their kids, and I put them up around the school. They were a huge hit.

Question 6: What do you want to do for and with your children to increase their chances of success—not just success in education but general success in the future?

Samuel: I am educating them while I am being educated. I am still growing. I am still trying to do well in life. As I am making different choices in life, I am trying to educate them, especially my oldest daughter. I tell her that I am doing these things because it is important to do them. After graduating from college, I'm going to other programs and getting different certifications. It is important that she sees her father doing these things. I also want to invest and put something in place so that my daughters will inherit some generational wealth. I have seen my in-laws do that. Now it's something I want to do with my children. Creating generational wealth begins with knowledge. Constantly being able to learn and constantly being able to communicate is key.

Thomas: That's a good question. My son has been honored with some of his good test scores. They did say that he learns faster than some other kids. He needs to be challenged. I definitely want to put some things in place where he is challenged. We recently got orders to relocate [*Authors' note:* Thomas's wife serves in the military], so it has opened my eyes to different things. When I was going to go to pick a new house, one of the first things that I looked into was the school system. What's the rating? I chose the area that we are going to be in so he can be challenged. I am definitely going to make sure he is in the right programs. I think that will go a long way. My dad did that for me. He challenged me when I was younger, so I am going to continue that as well. I don't want my son to look back and wish I had done things differently. I just want to keep him involved, keep him active, and keep him focused, and I think that will change his success in the future and give him a better opportunity, for sure.

David: I think one of the key parts is really walking along and staying present. The reason I say that is because a lot of time, our elders give us well-intended advice, but it just isn't relevant. We get advice for situations that no longer exist. If you're talking about home buying right now or finance right now, for example, they will say, "Why don't you save up and get a home?" That adage could be a deathtrap in some situations. Finance is the same thing; you can't leave your money in the bank, like we were always told. *Save your money in the bank*! Now we know money needs to be moving in order to grow. So, it's about continuing to walk alongside our kids and not just leave them alone to try to figure it out and critiquing what is happening from afar. Be the best model of health, which will increase their health outcomes. Mental health, too. My wife is a psychotherapist by trade, so taking our children's personal mental health seriously and making sure that the environment they are going to be in is prime—this is important. Actually, I started my mental health journey six months before my daughter was born. I didn't want her inheriting problems or anything that was unsolved. I wanted her to come into the best care as possible, and then we would figure it out from there. It's really about holding yourself accountable. The better you are, the better they can be.

Joseph: I will continue what my dad instilled in me. My dad did not grow up with a father. He had to learn the ropes as he was raising me. He taught me what he knew, so I have a better foundation than many. As David said, presence is important. I want to be present. I want to make sure my kids see me as I support them and help guide them. I want them to see my wife and me working together. I think Samuel said this, too: I want them to see me as vulnerable. When I make mistakes, it's important that they get a chance to see that . . . important that they know I don't always get it right. I make mistakes. I'm still learning, too. I don't know it all, but I know some things, and I'm going to share with them what I know.

Samuel: Echoing what David and Joseph said, investing in their future is one thing my wife and I talk about on a daily basis. I want our kids to have it a lot easier than we did. We have been blessed and highly favored to be in great families, but of course we want to take it to the next level as well—and why not? What's really big for me is being intentional about being present because I did not have a father growing up. I'm intentional about the little things. I'm intentional about being with my daughters to make sure that they *know* I am here and that they can feel it. My oldest daughter is at the age when she knows when I'm here and when I'm not here. There's been times where she could feel it that I was not engaged. I never want her to have that as a lasting feeling. I know the aftermath of what it is to feel that, so I don't want my daughters to feel that. I also feel that daughters feel things a little bit differently than boys do. You two can probably talk about that better than me. Just . . . the ladies feel that differently than guys.

Matthew: My children are high school through elementary. I am, like, the homework guy. Any time they need any help with their homework, like they have questions? They come to me. As soon as they get in the house, I check with them to find out what homework they have so we can get it going. It's the younger two I'm more on top of, obviously. The older two don't need me as much, but every now and then, they'll come and ask me or my wife for help for math or science. If it is math, I say, "Let's call for help." So, as a family, we don't play when it comes to that kind of stuff. My wife and I are there at the kitchen table with them, getting it done. To increase their chances of success, I will continue to make my presence known. I know that is one thing that I missed when I was younger. Simple things like a Senior Night and not having a dad there . . . things like that leave a mark. I just want them to know that I am always going to be here for them as long as I am on this earth. I think presence is a huge thing when it comes to children. Just seeing a father figure there is important, because it always seems like moms are there. I want them to know that Dad has their back, and anything they need in life I'm going to be there for them.

Question 7: The last question is what can schools and industries do to welcome you and your opinions into their spaces?

Samuel: Be active listeners. I think sometimes we as teachers, administrators, and even parents, we have these conversations where we are talking but we're not actively listening. It's important to listen, especially in these times when more and more children, young children, are frustrated. The time is now. We need action now. We must have the tough conversations that we are having right now. On both sides, everyone must rearrange their thought processes. We must change how we are working with and interacting with males. We also must look at how we have been taught some things and change those and rearrange those processes, too. This might be hard. When you've heard certain things for a long time, you think that may be the only way. It may be correct, but it may not be the only way. Be active listeners, but be aware that there is a bigger goal: to close the achievement gap and to push all kids so they are able to have the best benefits possible.

David: I think the conversation needs to continue to evolve. There is a diversity of parenting that needs to take place. We, as fathers, are seen as either secondary or absent but not as primary. We can start to partner with corporations and get the resources and programming we need to help us change that.

Joseph: I like the example that you gave—with the different fathers doing the READ posters for the schools and sharing books they read during games. That is not something that kids see often. Being an educator myself and knowing that the percentage of male educators is small, I think increasing opportunities for men in education is important. Increasing the presence of fathers in school and creating men's groups that would hold different activities maybe a couple times of a year where boys and girls can feel their presence . . . that's important, especially for kids who don't have that at home. I recently read about a situation in Louisiana, in a high school, where there was so much fighting. They called in a group of fathers to help out. The fathers stepped in, and just them being in the halls changed the school dramatically. The morale changed and the culture changed once the fathers took it upon themselves to make that change. How powerful the presence of fathers are. Something like that is needed. The opportunity to be in that space and for the students to see us.

Dr. Higdon: I have the framework for that. It's called the Fathers' Circle. I did it at the school where I previously worked. Fathers came in monthly and walked the building. It was extremely powerful.

Samuel: What David and Joseph said. Also just listening to us. Us being men. Sometimes—not sometimes, a lot of the times!—we are viewed as not knowing; we are viewed as uneducated and one-dimensional. Now more than ever, you see the shift. There is a shift and knowledge. There is a shift of men wanting to be immersed in all aspects of fatherhood. So just listening with an active ear to some of the things that are needed, such as men's presence, our accountability. That will help. Joseph, you know this, being in the school system. David and Matthew, you've both been in the school system, so you know this, too. You know kids look at us differently when they see us in an educational field or when they see you in the role of the lead teacher, the science teacher, the IT expert. Some people have never seen a man, especially one of color, in those positions. There are young men in my high school whom I try to mentor. I know that I'm a father figure to them. Granted, I am more like a big brother in age; however, I am still kind of like a father figure to them, because they have never had anyone to hold them accountable. That accountability aspect is key. They really just want that tough love, even when they recognize the tough part more than the love part. *Because I care about you, because I love you, we are having these courageous conversations.* We are wrapping our arms around them, and we are telling them that we love them. Because a lot of kids, especially young men, have never heard "I love you." That's key to the listening part. It's something that schools need to hear from Black men: We want to be there. We want to be prevalent, and we want to be respected, too.

Matthew: Schools need programs where men are seen. I can see from my children's friends asking them, "Oh, you have a dad in the house?" Now my kids realize that not all their friends have what they have at home. So, being in the schools and letting other kids know that dads are present—and not only do we care about our children, but we care about all the children. To have them see that someone cares about them, that a Black male cares about them, would be a huge thing, in my opinion. Samuel and I were lucky that in high school, our basketball coach was a Black man. Same thing with our football coach, which was something impactful in my life growing up: seeing Black men at the head of things through high school. They were great leaders. That was definitely something that motivated me. I think it would be something great for young kids to see. Not always with a coach but seeing their friends' parents coming in, talking to them, and having different programs with them. That would be major. Especially for the kids who won't speak up and let you know that they need that.

Peter: Clearer communication. We need daily communications sent home. The teachers need help, and we can help when they communicate with us about what is going on in class. If they need our help, ask for it.

Lucas: If you want us to help with homework, send home the lesson plan or directions. It's been years since some of us have been in school. We want to help, but we look at the directions and are confused. We can't ask the kids, because they are confused, too. It's hard for us to go and look at a sheet of paper without directions from teachers. Everyone has cell phones. Communicate with us via cell phones.

Benjamin: The teachers should have an understanding that every kid is not the same. Things are going on at home. They need to meet with parents and find out how each child learns and what they need. My daughter is too young for school, but I hope teachers will contact me and my wife so we can have a relationship with them. They need to let us know the best way to communicate with each other.

Conclusion

Dr. Abraham: Parenthood is difficult. As men, we need to express ourselves. It's all up here, in our heads: *I feel it, and I think it. I want to say it, but it doesn't come out.* I need to model the kind of father I want my son to be, the kind of husband I want my daughters to be attracted to. My younger child wants me to know she is there and wants to talk to me. The older two want that, too, but they don't want to talk to me necessarily. They want the security of my presence. Even if I am not doing anything, they want to know I am there. This role we play as men is so critical, so crucial. It's not easy to share from a male point of view the joys, the struggles, all that. There is a solidarity when we know we are speaking among one another.

David: My generation is taking to task this fatherhood thing, and everybody in my sphere, whether married or not, is putting the work in. Please amplify this. It's amazing.

Dr. Higdon: We want to get your voice, dads' voices, out there. You complete our work. You've been the missing part of the puzzle for years—purposefully and by mistake, in some cases. Now we need to purposefully engage you and bring you back again. We want this to be real, valuable, and authentic.

References

Amodia-Bidakowska, A., Laverty, C., & Ramchandani, P. G. (2020). Father–child play: A systemic review of its frequency, characteristics and potential impact on children's development. *Developmental Review, 100924*(57). https://doi.org/10.1016/j.dr.2020.100924

Annie E. Casey Foundation. (2023, February 13). Parental involvement vs. parental engagement [Blog post]. https://www.aecf.org/blog/parental-involvement-vs-parental-engagement

Astone, N., & Peters, E. (2014). Longitudinal influences on men's lives: Research from the Transition to Fatherhood Project and beyond. *Fathering*, 161–173. https://www.thefreelibrary.com/Longitudinal+influences+on+men%27s+lives%3a+research+from+the+transition... -a0381947379

Boberiene, L. V. (2013). Can policy facilitate human capital development? The critical role of student and family engagement in schools. *American Journal of Orthopsychiatry, 83*(2–3), 346–351.

Boudreau, E. (2020). *Effective family engagement starts with trust.* Harvard Graduate School of Education.

Braswell, K. (Director). (2014). *Spit'in anger*: *Venom of a fatherless son* [Film]. YouTube. Fathers Incorporated. https://www.youtube.com/watch?v=staKI0YX0Uc&list=PL18m34mX7F_Wsoh9xt-uB_4tWcZilmll1&index=3

Brooks, R., & Hodkinson, P. (2022). The distribution of educational labour in families with equal or primary care fathers. *British Journal of Sociology of Education, 43*(7), 995–1011.

Cabrera, N. J., Karberg, E., Malin, J. L., & Aldoney, D. (2017). The magic of play: Low-income mothers and fathers playfulness and children's emotion regulation and vocabulary skills. *Infant Mental Health Journal, 38*(6), 757–771.

Chism, D. (2022). *Leading your school toward equity: A practical framework for walking the talk*. ASCD.

Choi, R. (2023, February 23). The modern dad syndrome: Father figures in media. *The Berkley Beacon.* https://berkeleybeacon.com/the-modern-dad-syndrome-father-figures-in-media/

Coleman, J. S., Campbell, E. Q., Hobson, C. J., McPartland, J., Mood, A. M., Weinfeld, F. D., & York, R. L. (1966). *Equality of educational opportunity.* U.S. Department of Health, Education and Welfare, Office of Education. https://files.eric.ed.gov/fulltext/ED012275.pdf

Cramer, L., Goff, M., Peterson, B., & Sandstrom, H. (2017). *Parent–child visiting practices in prisons and jails: A synthesis of research and practice.* Urban Institute.

Cube. (2025, March 15). Building strong partnerships: 10 effective strategies for teachers to engage parents and guardians [Blog post]. *Cube for Teachers.* https://blog.cubeforteachers.com/partnerships/

Cullen, S. M., Cullen, M. A., & Lindsay, G. (2013). "I'm just there to ease the burden": The parent support advisor role in English schools and the question of emotional labour. *British Educational Research Journal, 39*(2), 302–318. https://doi.org/10.1080/01411926.2011.640393

DeGarmo, D. (2010). A time varying evaluation of identity theory and father involvement for full custody, shared custody, and no custody divorced fathers. *Fathering, 8,* 181–202.

Epstein, J. L., & Sanders, M. G. (2006). Prospects for change: Preparing educators for school, family, and community partnerships. *Peabody Journal of Education, 81*(2), 81–120.

Fanning, C. (2022, May 13). These fathers formed "Dads on Duty" to prevent violence at a local high school. *Reader's Digest.* https://www.rd.com/list/dads-on-duty

Fatherhood Project. (2023). *The state of fatherhood today (and why it matters to schools).* https://thefatherhoodproject.org/schools/the-research/

Ferguson, C. (2005). *Developing a collaborative team approach to support family and community connections with schools: What can school leaders do?* Southwest Educational Development Laboratory.

Fry, R. (2023). *Almost 1 in 5 stay-at-home parents in the U.S. are dads.* Pew Research Center. https://www.pewresearch.org/short-reads/2023/08/03/almost-1-in-5-stay-at-home-parents-in-the-us-are-dads/

Garbarino, J. (1999). *Lost boys: Why our sons turn violent and how we can save them.* Free Press.

Get Creative, Stay Connected. (2020). *Take time to be a dad today.* National Responsible Fatherhood Clearinghouse.

Green, B., Davis, C., Clark, T., Quinn, C., & Cryer-Coupet, Q. (2014). Father involvement, dating violence, and sexual risk behaviors among a national sample of adolescent females. *Journal of Interpersonal Violence, 31*(5), 810–830.

Head Start. (2025, May 5). Building partnerships with families [Online course]. https://www.headstart.gov/family-engagement/article/building-partnerships-families-course

Henderson, A. T. (1987). *The evidence continues to grow: Parent involvement improves student achievement.* National Committee for Citizens in Education.

Henderson, A. T., & Berla, N. (1994). *A new generation of evidence: The family is critical to student achievement.* Center for Law and Education.

Higgins, M. C. (2005). *Career imprints: Creating leaders across an industry.* Jossey-Bass.

Hohman-Marriott, B. (2011). Coparenting and father involvement in married and unmarried coresident couples. *Journal of Marriage and Family, 73*(1), 296–309.

Jackson, R. (2024, March 21). Mindsteps. LinkedIn. https://www.linkedin.com/in/robyn-jackson-mindsteps/

Kaufman, G. (2021). *Superdads: How fathers balance work and family in the 21st century.* NYU Press.

Kiviat, B. (2000, April). The social side of schooling. *Johns Hopkins Magazine.* https://pages.jh.edu/jhumag/0400web/18.html

Kotila, L. E., & Dush, C. (2013). Involvement with children and low-income fathers' psychological well-being. *Fathering, 11*(3), 306.

Lee, N. (2016, July 7). Narcotizing dysfunction: The danger of information. *Medium.* https://nicklee3.medium.com/narcotizing-dysfunction-the-danger-of-information-d832fd4869c0

Machin, A. (2019, December 10). *The science behind dads.* National Childbirth Trust. https://www.nct.org.uk/life-parent/bonding-and-caring-for-your-baby/science-behind-dads

Mapp, K., & Bergman, E. (2019). *Dual capacity-building framework for family–school partnerships.* Dual Capacity.

McBride, B. A., Schoppe-Sullivan, S. J., & Ho, M. (2005). The mediating role of fathers' involvement on student achievement. *Journal of Applied Developmental Psychology, 21,* 201–216.

McWayne, C., Downer, J. T., Campos, R., & Harris, R. D. (2013). Father involvement during early childhood and its association with children's early learning: A meta-analysis. *Early Education & Development, 24*(6), 898–922.

Miller, T. (2019). *Making sense of fatherhood: Gender, caring and work.* Cambridge University Press.

Mitchell, J. (2022, March 16). Don't ask, try inviting instead. *Hilborn: Charity eNews.* https://hilborn-charityenews.ca/articles/sns-dont-ask-try-inviting-instead

Montgomery County Public Schools. (2007, May 14). Kingsview fathers make a difference for African American students. *Staff Bulletin, 49*(35), 1, 8.

Murphy, A. P. (Host). (2016, February 24). Daddy, papi, papa, or baba: The influence of fathers on young children's development with Dr. Kyle Pruett (No. 290). *Zero to Three* [Audio podcast]. https://www.zerotothree.org/resources/290-the-influence-of-fathers-on-young-children-s-development

National Fatherhood Initiative. (n.d.). *30 ways to recruit dads into fatherhood programs.* https://www.fatherhood.org/championing-fatherhood/30-ways-to-recruit-dads-into-fatherhood-programs

National PTA. (2021). *PTA's leading the way in transformative family engagement.* https://www.pta.org/docs/default-source/files/membership/2021/nat-rep/ptas-leading-the-way-on-transformative-family-engagement.pdf

No Child Left Behind Act of 2001, P.L. 107–110, 20 U.S.C. § 6319 (2002).

Patton, A. (2012, November). A father–daughter dance . . . in prison. *TEDxWomen.* https://www.ted.com/talks/angela_patton_a_father_daughter_dance_in_prison/transcript

Pew Research Center. (2015). *Parenting in America: Outlook, worries, aspirations are strongly linked to financial situation.* https://www.pewresearch.org/wp-content/uploads/sites/3/2015/12/2015-12-17_parenting-in-america_FINAL.pdf

Phillips, D. (2023, February 21). The difference between inviting and asking. *Team Connections.* https://teamconnections.org/2023/02/21/the-difference-between-inviting-and-asking/

Pleck, J. H. (2010). Paternal involvement: Revised conceptualization and theoretical linkages with child outcomes. In M. E. Lamb (Ed.), *The role of the father in child development* (5th Ed., pp. 58–93). Wiley.

Pollack, W. (2000). *Real boys' voices.* Random House.

Scharrer, E. (2020, June 16). Why are sitcom dads still so inept? *The Conversation.* https://theconversation.com/why-are-sitcom-dads-still-so-inept-139737

Schoppe-Sullivan, S. (2017, February 2). Dads are more involved in parenting, yes, but moms still put in more work. *The Conversation.* https://www.theconversation.com/dads-are-more-involved-in-parenting-yes-but-moms-still-put-in-more-work-72026

Shreffler, K. M., Meadows, M. P., & Davis, K. D. (2011). Firefighting and fathering: Work–family conflict, parenting stress, and satisfaction with parenting and child behavior. *Fathering, 9,* 169–188.

Stringer, K. (2018, August 6). The 74 Interview: Harvard's Karen Mapp on ESSA, family engagement, and how schools and communities can partner to help kids succeed. *The 74.* https://www.the74million.org/article/the-74-interview-harvards-karen-mapp-on-essa-family-engagement-and-how-schools-and-communities-can-partner-to-help-kids-succeed

Tsoi-A-Fatt, R. (2010). *We dream a world: The 2025 vision for black men and boys.* Twenty-First Century Foundation.

U.S. Department of Education. (2024). *Let's talk back to school: Sample questions parents and families can ask to partner with your child's teachers and school.* Retrieved from https://www.ed.gov/sites/ed/files/2024-11/Let%E2%80%99s_Talk_Back_to_School_Eng_2024.pdf

Valenzuela, J. (2024, August 13). Beginning the school year with a consistent communication plan. *Edutopia.* https://www.edutopia.org/article/developing-good-communication-plan-students-families

Wallace, M. (2024, June 25). 60 parent engagement ideas to boost school improvement. *Possip.* https://possip.com/60-parent-engagement-ideas-to-boost-school-involvement/

Wirtz, P., & Schumacher, B. (2003). *Menu for successful parent and family involvement.* Southern Early Childhood Association.

Yeung, W. (2001). Children's time with fathers in intact families. *Journal of Marriage and Family, 63*(1), 136–152.

Index

The letter *f* following a page locator denotes a figure.

About the Authors

Chacko Abraham, EdD, is a husband, father of three, and an international educator, school administrator, writer, speaker, and school board and PTA member. His work focuses on how fathers can make a real difference in the lives of children, families, and schools. Having lived and worked in many countries, Abraham brings a global perspective to parenting, education, and family involvement. He draws from real classroom experiences and family life to show practical ways fathers can collaborate with teachers; participate in their children's learning; and show compassion, responsibility, and integrity.

Abraham writes for fathers who want to be present, professional educators who want stronger family partnerships, and communities that want to support the next generation. His work is based on the everyday realities of family life and the meaningful experience of watching children grow. Through storytelling, reflection, and practical advice, he encourages fathers to see their role not just as a responsibility but as a sacred calling, to lead with love, to be consistent, and to help their families feel rooted no matter where life takes them.

Abraham has a doctorate in education from the George Washington University and both his master's and undergraduate degrees in education from Temple University. He served as a professor at the Universidad de San Francisco de Quito in Ecuador.

Deborah R. Higdon, EdD, is an experienced educational leader. She has been a school nurse, high school teacher, assistant principal, principal, and central office supervisor. A father engagement specialist and a national and international speaker, she is currently a K–12 administrative substitute and an adjunct professor for Montgomery College, in Montgomery County, Maryland.

Twice, Higdon was selected as the principal of the year: once by the Montgomery County Public Schools media specialists and again by the Montgomery County Public Schools Junior Council, representing all the middle school students in the county. She is also a Claes Nobel Educator of Distinction awardee.

Higdon has a doctorate in educational leadership from Bowie State University, a master's degree in education from Hood College, and a Bachelor of Science from the University of Pittsburgh School of Nursing.

About ISTE+ASCD

ISTE+ASCD's mission is to empower educators to reimagine and redesign learning through impactful pedagogy and meaningful technology use. We achieve this by offering transformative professional learning, cultivating and disseminating thought leadership, fostering vibrant communities, and ensuring that digital tools and experiences are accessible and effective.

Related Books and Resources

At the time of publication, the following resources related to this book's topic were available:

The Consciously Unbiased Educator by Huda Essa (Book)

Every Connection Matters: How to Build, Maintain, and Restore Relationships Inside the Classroom and Out by Michael Creekmore and Nita Creekmore (Book)

Everyday Engagement: Making Students and Parents Your Partners in Learning by Katy Ridnouer (Book)

Meet Their Needs, and They'll Succeed: Transforming Students' Lives Through Positive Relationships by Salome Thomas-EL (Book)

The Six Priorities: How to Find the Resources Your School Community Needs by Luis Eladio Torres (Book)

Stay and Prevail: Students of Color Don't Need to Leave Their Communities to Succeed by Nancy Gutiérrez & Roberto Padilla (Book)

The Teens Are Not Alright: School and Classroom Practices to Support Student Well-Being by Cathy Vatterott (Book)

For up-to-date information about ISTE+ASCD resources, go to iste-ascd.org/books-and-publications. To learn more about membership and join or renew, go to iste-ascd.org/membership, email memsupport@iste-ascd.org, or call 1-800-933-2723 or 703-578-9600.

www.ingramcontent.com/pod-product-compliance
Lightning Source LLC
LaVergne TN
LVHW010108170826
845678LV00012B/2304

* 9 7 8 1 4 1 6 6 3 4 3 3 1 *